THE ROYAL COURT
THEATRE PRESENTS

HOW TO HOLD YOUR BREATH

BY ZINNIE HARRIS

How to Hold Your Breath was first
performed at the Royal Court Jerwood
Theatre Downstairs, Sloane Square, on
Wednesday 4 February 2015.

HOW TO HOLD YOUR BREATH
BY ZINNIE HARRIS

CAST (in order of appearance)

Dana **Maxine Peake**
Jarron **Michael Shaeffer**
Jasmin **Christine Bottomley**
Interviewer/Doctor/Clara **Danusia Samal**
Interviewer/Marta/Telephone Operator **Siobhán McSweeney**
Interviewer/Train Inspector/Punter **Neil D'Souza**
Librarian **Peter Forbes**

Also includes
Joshua Campbell
Raghad Chaar
Soledad Delahoz
Marisa Flamino
Michael Jinks
Djordje Jovanovic
Connor Mills

Mark Ota
Aaron Peters
Alison Porter
Ruth Pugh
Javier Rasero
Jessica Simet
Ben Tiramani
Temi Wilkey

Director **Vicky Featherstone**
Designer **Chloe Lamford**
Lighting Designer **Paule Constable**
Composer **Stuart Earl**
Sound Designer **Gareth Fry**
Movement Director **Ann Yee**
Assistant Director **Debbie Hannan**
Casting Director **Amy Ball**
Production Manager **Niall Black**
Costume Supervisor **Lucy Walshaw**
Stage Manager **Joni Carter**
Deputy Stage Manager **Fiona Kennedy**
Assistant Stage Manager **Heather Cryan**
Stage Management Work Placement **Beth McKnight**
Set constructed by **MDM Props Ltd & Weld-Fab Stage Engineering Ltd**

The Royal Court wish to thank the following for their help with this production:
Books for Free, Foyles Charing Cross Road, Goldboro Books, Waterstones Charing Cross.

HOW TO HOLD YOUR BREATH
THE COMPANY

Zinnie Harris (Writer)

For the Royal Court: **Nightingale & Chase.**

Other theatre includes: **The Message, On the Watch, The Panel (Tricycle); The Wheel (National Theatre of Scotland/ Steppenwolf Theatre Company, Chicago); The Garden, Fall (Traverse); Solstice, Midwinter (RSC); Further than the Furthest Thing (National/Tron); By Many Wounds (Hampstead).**

Adaptations include: **A Doll's House (Donmar); Miss Julie (National Theatre of Scotland).**

Television includes: **Born With Two Mothers, Richard is my Boyfriend, Spooks, Partners in Crime.**

Opera includes: **The Garden (Sound Festival Scotland); Death of a Scientist (Scottish Opera).**

Awards include: **Amnesty International Freedom of Expression Theatre Award (The Wheel); Arts Foundation Fellowship Award (Midwinter); Peggy Ramsey Writing Award (Further than the Furthest Thing); John Whiting Award (Further than the Furthest Thing); & several Fringe First Awards.**

Zinnie is currently under commission to the Royal Shakespeare Company and the National Theatre of Scotland. From April 2015 she will working as the Associate Director of the Traverse Theatre.

Christine Bottomley (Jasmine)

For the Royal Court: **Alaska, Ladybird.**

Other theatre includes: **Uncle Vanya (Young Vic); Osama the Hero, A Single Act (Hampstead); Flush (Soho); Rutherford & Son (Royal Exchange, Manchester); The Pleasure Man (Citizens).**

Television includes: **Cucumber, In the Club, Undeniable, Moving On, DCI Banks, The Street, Great Night Out, Frankie, Vera, Silent Witness, Secrets & Words, The Secret Diaries of Miss Anne Lister, The Land Girls, Hope Springs, Tess of the D'Urbervilles, New Tricks, Inspector George Gentley, Midsomer Murders, Massive, Torchwood, The Palace, Survivors, Sea of Souls, Sound, Instinct, The Innocence Project, The Preston Passion, Blue Murder, Simon Schama: Power of Art, Vincent, Shameless, Murder Prevention, Early Doors, Grease Monkeys, Speeding, Sex, Footballers & Videotape, Heatbeat, Dalziel & Pascoe, The Inspector Lynley Mysteries, EastEnders.**

Film includes: **Keeping Rosy, The Arbor, Strawberry Fields, All in Good Time, Hush, Lost Christmas, The Waiting Room, Venus.**

Radio includes: **Dream of White Horses, Man in the Moon, Treats, My Boy, The House of Bernada Alba, Tony Teardrop, Everyone Quite Likes Justin, The Dark Side, Money Magic, Scissors & Ribbon.**

Awards include: **BBC Audio Drama Award for Best Actress (My Boy).**

Paule Constable (Lighting Designer)

For the Royal Court: **Clybourne Park, Posh, The City, Krapps Last Tape, Forty Winks, Boy Gets Girl, Night Songs, The Country, Dublin Carol, The Weir (&West End/ Broadway).**

Theatre includes: **Behind the Beautiful Forevers, The Light Princess, Table, This House, The Curious Incident of the Dog in the Night Time, Phedre, Death and the King's Horseman, War Horse (& West End/ Broadway/US tour); Saint Joan, Waves, His Dark Materials, (National); Wolf Hall (& West End/Broadway); The Prince of Homburg, The Seagull, Tales from Ovid, The Dispute, Uncle Vanya, The Mysteries (RSC); Luise Miller, Ivanov (Donmar/West End); The Chalk Garden, Othello (Donmar); Happy Days, Feast, The Good Soul of Szechaun, Generations, Vernon God Little (Young Vic); Blasted, Three Sisters (Lyric, Hammersmith); Don Carlos (Crucible, Sheffield/West End); A Midsummer Night's Dream, Peter & Alice, The Cripple of Inishmaan, Privates on Parade, (Michael Grandage Co); Moon for the Misbegotten, Dancing at Lughnasa (Old Vic).**

Opera includes: **Carmen, Faust, Rigoletto, The Marriage of Figaro, The Magic Flute, Macbeth (ROH); The Marriage of Figaro, The Cunning Little Vixen, Die Meistersinger, Billy Budd, Rusalka, St Matthew Passion, Cosi Fan Tutte, Giulio Cesare, Carmen, The Double Bill, La Boheme (Glyndebourne); Cosi fan Tutte, Bienvenuto Cellini, Medea, Idomeneo, Satyagraha, Clemenza Di Tito, Gotterdamerung, The Rape of Lucretia, Manon (ENO); Peter Grimes (Opera North); The Marriage of Figaro, The Merry Widow, Don Giovanni, Anna Bolena (The Metropolitan, New York); Tales of Hoffman (Salzburg Festival); Poppea (Theatre Champs Elysees); Agrippina, A Midsummer Night's Dream, Cosi, The Ring Cycle (Opera National du Rhin);**

Tristan und Isolde (New National Opera, Tokyo).

Dance includes: **The Goldberg Variations (Kim Brandstrup); Seven Deadly Sins (Royal Ballet); Naked (Ballet Boyz); Sleeping Beauty, Dorian Gray, Play Without Words (Matthew Bourne).**

Paule has been the recipient of 4 Olivier Awards, a Tony Award and both the LA and New York Critics Circle Awards. She is an associate at the National Theatre.

Neil D'Souza (Interviewer/Train Inspector/Punter)

For the Royal Court: **Khandan.**

Other theatre includes: **Drawing the Line (Hampstead); Much Ado About Nothing, Midnight's Children (RSC); Protozoa, Oikos (The Red Room); Tintin (West End/tour); The Man of Mode (National); Our Country's Good, A Midsummer Night's Dream (Mercury, Colchester); Twelfth Night (Albery); Richard III (Haymarket, Leicester); The Merchant of Venice, The Honest Whore (Globe); The Merchant of Venice (English Shakespeare); Staying On (Theatre of Comedy); A Little Princess (Library).**

Television includes: **Cut, Raised by Wolves, Citizen Khan, Friday Night Dinner, Doctors, Albert's Memorial, Hustle, The Bill, Happiness, Absolutely True, Back Up.**

Film includes: **Another Me, Still Life, Closed Circuit, Jadoo, Filth, Naachle London, Italian Movies, Wild Target, Gateway to Heaven, Ganga Guest House, The Late Twentieth, My Sweet Home, Love Letters.**

Radio includes: **Recent Events at Collington House, Ask Mina, Goan Flame, The Red Oleander.**

Stuart Earl (Composer)

For the Royal Court: **Routes.**

Other theatre includes: **A Doll's House (Young Vic/West End/BAM, New York); Blurred Lines (National); Candida (Theatre Royal, Bath); Regeneration (Royal & Derngate).**

Television includes: **Babylon, Mayday, Black Mirror: The Entire History of You.**

Film includes: **Lilting, My Brother the Devil, In Our Name, Guilty Pleasures.**

Vicky Featherstone (Director)

For the Royal Court: **God Bless the Child, Maidan: Voices from the Uprising, The Mistress Contract, The Ritual Slaughter of Gorge Mastromas, Untitled Matriarch Play, The President Has Come to See You** (Open Court Weekly Rep).

Other theatre includes: **Enquirer (co-director), An Appointment with the Wicker Man, 27, The Wheel, Somersaults, Wall of Death: A Way of Life (co-director) The Miracle Man, Empty, Long Gone Lonesome (National Theatre of Scotland) Cockroach (National Theatre of Scotland Traverse); 365 (National Theatre of Scotland/Edinburgh International Festival); Mary Stuart (National Theatre of Scotland/Citizens/Royal Lyceum, Edinburgh); The Wolves in the Walls (co-director) (National Theatre of Scotland/Improbable/Tramway/Lyric, Hammersmith/UK tour/New Victory, New York); The Small Things, Pyrenees, The Drowned World, Tiny Dynamite, Crazy Gary's Mobile Disco, Splendour, Riddance The Cosmonaut's Last Message to the Woman He Once Loved in the Former Soviet Union, Crave (Paines Plough).**

Created for television: **Where the Heart Is, Silent Witness.**

Vicky was Artistic Director of Paines Plough 1997–2005 and the founding Artistic Director of The National Theatre of Scotland 2005–2012.

Vicky is the Artistic Director of the Royal Court.

Peter Forbes (Librarian)

Theatre includes: **The James Plays (National Theatre of Scotland/National); The Same Deep Water as Me (Donmar) Singin' in the Rain (West End/Chichester Festival); Educating Agnes (Lyceum, Edinburgh); Diary of a Nobody, Travels with My Aunt (Royal & Derngate); The Three Musketeers & The Princess of Spain (ETT/Traverse); Treasure Island (Rose, Kingston); The Observer, Afterlife, Never So Good, Two Weeks with the Queen (National); Black Watch (National Theatre of Scotland/Broadway/Dublin/tour); Donkeys' Years (UK tour); A Journey to London, Adam Bede (Orange Tree); The Winter's Tale, Troilus & Cressida (Globe); My Dad's A Birdman (Young Vic); Singin' in the Rain (Sadler's Wells); A Midsummer Night's Dream, Twelfth Night, A Funny Thing Happened on the Way to the Forum, The Comedy of Errors, The Tempest (Regent's Park Open Air); Mamma Mia! (West End); A Small Family Business (Chichester Festival); The Duchess of Malfi (Mercury Colchester); Richard III, Aladdin, Juno & The Paycock, Guys & Dolls (Haymarket, Leicester); A Word from our Sponsor (Scarborough/Chichester Festival).**

Television includes: **Holby City, Doctors, The Promise, The First Men in the Moon,**

EastEnders, Taggart, Little Devil, Bad Girls, The Bill, A Touch of Frost, The Government Inspector, Casualty, The English Revolution, Walking on the Moon, The Stalker's Apprentice, Berkeley Square.

Films include: **Nativity 3, Wilde, Blue Ice.**

Radio includes: **The Architects, Burns & the Bankers, Black Watch, Beryl Du Jour, Two Weeks with the Queen, Raffles.**

Gareth Fry (Sound Designer)

For the Royal Court: **Let the Right One In (& National Theatre of Scotland/West End), Truth & Reconcilliation, Wastwater, Chicken Soup with Barley, The City.**

Theatre includes: **Wilde Fire (Hampstead), The Cherry Orchard (Young Vic); John (DV8/National); Dusk (Fevered Sleep); Othello (Frantic Assembly); Fully Committed (Menier Chocolate Factory); The Forbidden Zone (Schaubühne, Berlin); A Small Family Business, Othello, The Cat in the Hat, A Matter Of Life & Death (& Kneehigh), Attempts on Her Life, Waves (National); David Bowie Is (V&A/tour); The Master & Margarita, Shun-kin, Endgame (Complicite), Black Watch (National Theatre of Scotland); The Secret Agent (Theatre O), The Noise (Unlimited), Trojan Women (Gate), Wild Swans, Hamlet (Young Vic), Reise Durch die Nacht (Schauspiel, Cologne), Richard III (Old Vic/BAM, New York/International tour); Die Gelde Tapete, Fraulein Julie (Schabühne, Berlin).**

Television includes: **CBeebies Christmas Carol.**

Radio includes: **Jump, OK Computer, The Overwhelming.**

Events include: **Somerset House Film4 Summer Screen & Ice Rink, Five Stages of Truth (V&A), Digital Revolution (Barbican Curve), Soundscape Design, Opening Ceremony of the 2012 Olympic Games.**

Awards include: **Olivier Award for Sound Design (Waves); Helpmann Award for Sound Design (Black Watch) Olivier Award for Sound Design (Black Watch); IRNE Award for Sound Design (Wild Swans).**

Debbie Hannan (Assistant Director)

As Director, for the Royal Court: **Spaghetti Ocean, Peckham: The Soap Opera (co-director).**

As Assistant Director, for the Royal Court: **God Bless the Child, Teh Internet is Serious Business, The Nether, Primetime, Birdland, The Mistress Contract.**

As Director, other theatre includes: **Notes from the Underground (Citizens); Panorama, Roses Are Dead, You Cannot Call it Love (Arches); Yellow Pears (Swept Up); liberty, equality, fraternity (Tron/Traverse).**

As Associate Director, other theatre includes: **Little on the Inside (Clean Break).**

As Assistant Director, other theatre includes: **A Doll's House, Enquirer (National Theatre of Scotland/Royal Lyceum, Edinburgh); The Maids, Beauty & the Beast (Citizens); Kurt Weill: Double Bill (Scottish Opera); War of the Roses Trilogy (Bard in the Botanics); Hamlet (Globe Education).**

Debbie is Trainee Director at the Royal Court.

Chloe Lamford (Designer)

For the Royal Court: **God Bless the Child, 2071, Teh Internet is Serious Business, Open Court, Circle Mirror Transformation.**

Other theatre includes: **Salt Root & Roe (Donmar/Trafalgar Studios); Praxis Makes Perfect (National Theatre Wales); Lungs (Schaubühne, Berlin); 1984 (Headlong/Almeida/West End/tour); Rules for Living, The World of Extreme Happiness (National); Boys (Headlong); Cannibals, The Gate Keeper (Royal Exchange, Manchester); The Events (Actors Touring Company/Young Vic/tour); The History Boys (Crucible, Sheffield); Disco Pigs, Sus, Blackta (Young Vic); My Shrinking Life, An Appointment With the Wicker Man, Knives in Hens (National Theatre of Scotland); The Radicalisation of Bradley Manning (National Theatre Wales/Edinburgh International Festival); Ghost Story (Sky Arts Live Drama); Britannicus (Wilton's Music Hall); My Romantic History (Crucible, Sheffield/Bush); Joseph K, The Kreutzer Sonata (Gate); Songs From A Hotel Bedroom (ROH/tour); it felt empty when the heart went at first but it is alright now, This Wide Night (Clean Break); The Mother Ship, How to Tell the Monsters from the Misfits (Birmingham Rep); Small Miracle (Tricycle/Mercury, Colchester).**

Awards Include: **Theatrical Management Association Award for Best Theatre Design (Small Miracle); Arts Foundation Fellowship Award for Design for Performance: Set & Costume.**

Siobhán McSweeney (Interviewer/Marta/Telephone Operator)

Theatre includes: **Fathers & Sons (Donmar); The Captain of Köpenick, The Kitchen, Mother Courage & Her Children, England**

People Very Nice (National); Uncle Vanya (Lyric, Belfast); Translations (Curve, Leicester); Dancing at Lughnasa (Birmingham Rep); The Flags (Royal Exchange, Manchester); Midden (Oldham Coliseum).

Television includes: **The Fall, No Offence, London Irish.**

Film includes: **The Wind that Shakes the Barley, Alice in Wonderland: Alice Through the Looking Glass.**

Awards include: **Manchester Evening News Award for Best Studio Performance (The Flags).**

Maxine Peake (Dana)

For the Royal Court: **Mother Teresa is Dead.**

Other theatre includes: **Hamlet, Miss Julie, The Children's Hour, Rutherford & Sons (Royal Exchange, Manchester); The Masque of Anarchy (Manchester International Festival); Loyalty (Hampstead); The Deep Blue Sea, Hamlet (West Yorkshire Playhouse); Leaves of Glass (Soho); On the Third Day, Miss Julie (West End); Robin Hood, Luther, The Relapse, The Cherry Orchard (National); Sergeant Musgrave's Dance (Oxford Stage); Early One Morning (Octagon).**

Television includes: **The Village, Silk, Henry IV, Room at the Top, The Secret Diaries of Miss Anne Lister, Criminal Justice, The Street, Marple, Red Riding 1980, Hancock & Joan, Little Dorrit, The Devil's Whore, Bike Squad, Cinderella, Confessions of a Diary Secretary, See No Evil, Faith, Shameless, Christmas Lights, Early Doors, The Way We Live Now, Victoria Wood & All the Trimmings, Dinnerladies, Clocking Off.**

Film includes: **The Falling, The Theory of Everything, Keeping Rosie, Run & Jump, Svengali, Private Peaceful, Best Laid Plans, Edge, Clubbed, All or Nothing, Girls Night.**

Awards include: **Manchester Theatre Award for Best Actress (Miss Julie); RTS North Award for Best Actress (See No Evil); Manchester Evening News Theatre Award for Best Actress (The Children's Hour).**

Danusia Samal (Interviewer/ Doctor/Clara)

Theatre includes: **Circles (Birmingham Rep/Tricycle); The House That Will Not Stand (Tricycle); Billy the Girl (Clean Break/Soho); Finding Noor (Citizens); The Birthday Party (Royal Exchange, Manchester); 1001 Nights (Unicorn/ Transport); Liar Liar (Unicorn); A**

Mother's Will (StoneCrabs); After the Rainfall (Curious Directive).

Television includes: **Boom!.**

Film includes: **In Close Quarters, Do You Want to Try Again?.**

Michael Shaeffer (Jarron)

For the Royal Court: **Open Court.**

Other theatre includes: **Little Revolution, Mr Burns (Almeida); Godchild (Hampstead); Table, London Road, The Threepenny Opera (& UK tour) (National); The Merry Wives of Windsor, Twelfth Night (Stafford Castle); All About My Mother (Old Vic); Restoration (Oxford Stage Company); Of Mice And Men (Mercury, Colchester); Hamlet (Northampton Royal); Dreams From a Summerhouse (Watermill, Newbury); Original Sin (Crucible, Sheffield); Macbeth (Southwark); The Beautiful Game (West End); Jesus Christ Superstar (UK tour).**

Television includes: **New Tricks, Foyle's War, Luther, Black Mirror, Mrs Biggs, Parade's End, Game of Thrones, Silent Witness, M High, Kings & Queens, EastEnders, World in Arms – Navies.**

Film includes: **London Road, London Fields, Broken, Anna Karenina, Trance, Gullive Travels, Breaking & Entering, Kingdom Heaven.**

Radio includes: **For Services Rendered, Births, Marriages & Deaths.**

Ann Yee (Movement Director)

Theatre includes: **Urinetown (St. James'); Blurred Lines, She Stoops to Conquer, The Comedy of Errors (National); The Commitments (West End); The Color Purple, Torch Song Trilogy (Menier Chocolate Factory); Macbeth (Trafalgar Studios); Henry IV, Julius Caesar, Berenice, Philadelphia, Here I Come!, The 25th Annual Putnam County Spelling Bee (Donmar Warehouse); The Accrington Pals, The Country Wife (Roy Exchange, Manchester); The Duchess o Malfi (Old Vic); After Miss Julie (Young Vic); King Lear, A Soldier in Every Son (RSC); Orpheus, Eurydice (NYT at Old Vic Tunnels); Salome (Headlong); Much Ado About Nothing (Regent's Park Open Air); Eric's (Liverpool Everyman).**

Opera includes: **Wozzeck (ENO), Ingerland (ROH).**

THE ROYAL COURT THEATRE

The Royal Court Theatre is the writers' theatre. It is the leading force in world theatre for energetically cultivating writers – undiscovered, new, and established.

Through the writers the Royal Court is at the forefront of creating restless, alert, provocative theatre about now, inspiring audiences and influencing future writers. Through the writers the Royal Court strives to constantly reinvent the theatre ecology, creating theatre for everyone.

We invite and enable conversation and debate, allowing writers and their ideas to reach and resonate beyond the stage, and the public to share in the thinking.

Over 120,000 people visit the Royal Court in Sloane Square, London, each year and many thousands more see our work elsewhere through transfers to the West End and New York, national and international tours, residencies across London and site-specific work.

The Royal Court's extensive development activity encompasses a diverse range of writers and artists and includes an ongoing programme of writers' attachments, readings, workshops and playwriting groups. Twenty years of pioneering work around the world means the Royal Court has relationships with writers on every continent.

The Royal Court opens its doors to radical thinking and provocative discussion, and to the unheard voices and free thinkers that, through their writing, change our way of seeing.

Within the past sixty years, John Osborne, Arnold Wesker and Howard Brenton have all started their careers at the Court. Many others, including Caryl Churchill, Mark Ravenhill and Sarah Kane have followed. More recently, the theatre has found and fostered new writers such as Polly Stenham, Mike Bartlett, Bola Agbaje, Nick Payne and Rachel De-lahay and produced many iconic plays from Laura Wade's **Posh** to Bruce Norris' **Clybourne Park** and Jez Butterworth's **Jerusalem**. Royal Court plays from every decade are now performed on stage and taught in classrooms across the globe.

It is because of this commitment to the writer that we believe there is no more important theatre in the world than the Royal Court.

Supported using public funding by
ARTS COUNCIL ENGLAND

ROYAL COURT SUPPORTERS

The Royal Court is a registered charity and not-for-profit company. We need to raise £1.7 million every year in addition to our core grant from the Arts Council and our ticket income to achieve what we do.

We have significant and longstanding relationships with many generous organisations and individuals who provide vital support. Royal Court supporters enable us to remain the writers' theatre, find stories from everywhere and create theatre for everyone.

We can't do it without you.

Innovation partner

Supported using public funding by
ARTS COUNCIL
ENGLAND

EMPLOYEES
THE ROYAL COURT & ENGLISH STAGE COMPANY

Artistic Director
Vicky Featherstone
Executive Producer
Lucy Davies

Associate Directors
**Hamish Pirie, John
Tiffany*, Lucy Morrison***
Artistic Associates
**Ola Animashawun*,
Emily McLaughlin***
Associate Artist
Chloe Lamford*
Trainee Director
Debbie Hannan‡
Associate Artists
**Carrie Cracknell, Simon
Godwin, Katie Mitchell**
International Director
Elyse Dodgson
International Associate
Richard Twyman
International Administrator
Callum Smith*
Education Associate
Lynne Gagliano*
Education Apprentice
Maia Clarke

Literary Manager
Christopher Campbell
Deputy Literary Manager
Louise Stephens
Literary Administrator
Hayley Dallimore
Trainee Administrator
(Literary)
Ashiokai Omaboe§

Head of Casting
Amy Ball
Casting Associate
Louis Hammond

Head of Production
Niall Black
Production Manager
Tariq Rifaat
Production Assistant
Zoe Hurwitz
Head of Lighting
Jack Williams
Deputy Head of Lighting
Marec Joyce
Lighting Technicians
**Jess Faulks,
Matthew Harding**
JTD Programmer & Operator
Laura Whitley

Head of Stage
Steven Stickler
Stage Deputy
Dan Lockett
Stage Chargehand
Lee Crimmen
Chargehand & Building
Maintenance Technician
Matt Livesey
Head of Sound
David McSeveney
Sound & Video Deputy
Emily Legg
Sound Operator
Madison English
Technical Trainee
Ashley Lednor§
Head of Costume
Lucy Walshaw
Wardrobe Deputy
Gina Lee

General Manager
**Catherine
Thornborrow**
Administrator
(Maternity Leave)
Holly Gladwell
Administrator
(Maternity Cover)
Minna Sharpe
Projects Manager
Chris James
Assistant to the Executive
Phoebe Eclair-Powell
Trainee Administrator
(Producing)
Cherrelle Glaves§
Associate Producer
Daniel Brodie*
Community Producer
(Pimlico)
Chris Sonnex*
Community Producer
(Tottenham)
Adjoa Wiredu*
Finance Director
Helen Perryer
Finance Manager
Martin Wheeler
Finance Officer
Rachel Harrison*
Finance & Administration
Assistant
Rosie Mortimer

Head of Marketing
& Sales
Becky Wootton
Press & Public Relations
The Cornershop PR
Marketing Manager
Dion Wilson
Communications Trainees
**Katie Davison§, Rida
Hamidou§**

Sales Manager
Liam Geoghegan
Deputy Sales Manager
Sarah Murray
Box Office Sales
Assistants
**Ryan Govin, Joe
Hodgson, Helen
Preddy* (Maternity
Leave), Margaret
Perry* (Maternity
Cover)**

Head of Development
(Maternity Leave)
Rebecca Kendall
Head of Development
(Maternity Cover)
Lucy Buxton
Senior Individual Giving
Manager
Sue Livermore*
Trusts & Foundations
Manager
Clare O'Hara*
Development Managers
**Luciana Lawlor,
Anna Sampson**
Development Officer
Nadia Vistisen

Theatre Manager
Rachel Dudley
Senior Duty House
Manager
Maureen Huish
Theatre Assistant
Chris Sonnex*
Venue Operations
Apprentice
Naomi Wright
Duty House Managers
**Florence Bourne,
Elinor Keber, Tanya
Shields**
Bar & Kitchen Manager
Ali Christian
Deputy Bar &
Kitchen Manager
Robert Smael
Assistant Bar &
Kitchen Manager
Jared Thomas
Head Chef
Tim Jenner
Sous Chef
Mandy Fitzhugh

Bookshop Manager
Simon David
Bookshop Assistant
Vanessa Hammick*

Stage Door/Reception
**Paul Lovegrove,
Tyrone Lucas,
Jane Wainwright**

Thanks to all of our Ushers
and Bar & Kitchen staff.

§ Posts supported by
The Sackler Trust
Trainee Scheme
‡The post of Trainee
Director is supported
by an anonymous donor.
* Part-time.

ENGLISH STAGE
COMPANY

President
**Dame Joan
Plowright CBE**

Remember the Royal Court in your will and help to ensure that our future is as iconic as our past

Every gift, whatever the amount, will help us maintain and care for the building, support the next generation of playwrights starting out in their career, deliver our education programme and put our plays on the stage.

LEAVE A LEGACY

To discuss leaving a legacy to the Royal Court please contact:

Anna Sampson, Development Manager,
Royal Court Theatre, Sloane Square,
London, SW1W 8AS

Email: annasampson@royalcourttheatre.com
Tel: 020 7565 5049

How to Hold Your Breath

Zinnie Harris's plays include the multi-award-winning *Further than the Furthest Thing*, produced by the National Theatre/Tron Theatre in 2000 (1999 Peggy Ramsay Playwriting Award, 2001 John Whiting Award, Edinburgh Festival Fringe First award); *Nightingale and Chase* (Royal Court Theatre, 2001); and *By Many Wounds* (Hampstead Theatre, 1999). *Solstice*, the first in a trilogy of plays, was staged in 2005 by the RSC, who had already presented *Midwinter* in 2004; the last, *Fall*, was staged at the Traverse, Edinburgh, in 2008. *The Wheel* was staged at the Traverse Theatre by the National Theatre of Scotland and was joint winner of the Amnesty International Freedom of Expression Award 2011. Zinnie Harris has received an Arts Foundation Fellowship for playwriting, and was Writer in Residence at the RSC, 2000–2001. She is a part-time Senior Lecturer in playwriting at St Andrews University, and from April 2015 will be an Associate Director at the Traverse Theatre.

ZINNIE HARRIS

How to Hold Your Breath

ff

FABER & FABER

First published in 2015
by Faber and Faber Ltd
74–77 Great Russell Street
London WC1B 3DA

Typeset by Country Setting, Kingsdown, Kent CT14 8ES
Printed in England by CPI Group (UK) Ltd, Croydon CR0 4YY

A CIP record for this book
is available from the British Library

978-0-571-32492-7

2 4 6 8 10 9 7 5 3 1

Thanks to the following:

Nikki Amuka-Bird, Pippa Bennett-Warner,
Adam Best, Vera Chok, Darrell D'Silva,
Sam Troughton, Debbie Hannan, John Harris,
Mark and Fran Shaw, Frances Poet,
Dinah Wood, Steve King and Mel Kenyon.

Above all thanks to Vicky Featherstone –
collaborator, encourager, inspiration and friend.

How to Hold Your Breath was first performed at the Royal Court Jerwood Theatre Downstairs, London, on 4 February 2015. The cast was as follows:

Dana Maxine Peake
Jarron Michael Shaeffer
Jasmin Christine Bottomley
Interviewer / Doctor / Clara Danusia Samal
Interviewer / Marta / Telephone Operator
    Siobhán McSweeney
Interviewer / Train Inspector / Punter Neil D'Souza
Librarian Peter Forbes
Ensemble Joshua Campbell, Raghad Chaar,
    Soledad Delahoz, Marisa Flamino, Michael Jinks,
    Djordje Jovanovic, Connor Mills, Mark Ota,
    Aaron Peters, Alison Porter, Ruth Pugh, Javier Rasero,
    Jessica Simet, Ben Tiramani, Temi Wilkey

Director Vicky Featherstone
Designer Chloe Lamford
Lighting Designer Paule Constable
Composer Stuart Earl
Sound Designer Gareth Fry
Movement Director Ann Yee
Assistant Director Debbie Hannan

Characters

Dana
a woman in her late twenties

Jarron
a man who works for the UN

Jasmine
Dana's sister

Librarian
a book worm

Train Inspector

Woman
telephone operator

Punter
a man looking for sex

Marta
a woman who used to be on TV

Clara
a woman who used to be a lawyer

Doctor

The Interview Panel
three voices

HOW TO HOLD YOUR BREATH

for my sister

ONE

Dana speaks to the audience.

Dana
I am stand at the back. Don't look out. Gets shouted
at for looking down. I am eyes closed, head bent in
every gathering. I am knees bowed, chest to the floor.
I am a flower by the wall, grass in the shade. I am
back turned, shoulders hunched, face hollowed. I am
a scream. A howl. I am a snake on the plane, a hyena,
an antelope. I am ant under a stone, beetle scurrying
away. I am beaten at birth, blackened. I am sand. I am
soil. I am earth. I am less than earth. I am poor. I'm so
poor my skin is my clothes. I am uncovered. Ashamed.
The land can't feed me. I am the end. The dead. The
carcass by the roadside. I am the abyss into which
people dread to fall.

She stops and looks at herself in the mirror.

She takes a deep breath.

TWO

Europe.

*In a cosy room two lovers lie under the covers intertwined
and heavy with sleep. The woman, Dana, is in her late
twenties. The man, Jarron, is a little older.*

Dana sits up.

Jarron
don't do that

Dana
I had such a strange dream

Jarron
it's not even morning yet

Dana
but the sun's up

Beat.

hey the sun's up

Jarron
so the sun's up, we can sleep a bit longer, can't we?

Dana
we could

Jarron
then why don't we?

He pulls her back down.

She laughs.

He covers her with the sheet.

She lets him.

He kisses her.

She kisses him back.

Dana
you've got a scar on your chest

Jarron
that was where they ripped my soul out.

Dana
very funny.

They kiss again.

He rolls on top of her.

Dana
actually I'm quite hungry

Jarron
what?

Dana
aren't you?
I mean don't you want something to eat?

Jarron
not particularly

Dana
don't you eat where you come from?

Jarron
sometimes but not in the middle of –

Dana
have some fruit then, some bread
it's breakfast time

Jarron
seriously?

Dana
seriously
I'm starving.

Jarron
alright. What do you have?

Dana
what do you want?

Jarron
what have you got?

Dana
there's a shop downstairs
anything you can imagine

Jarron
they're open at this time?

Dana
it's not early. It's getting late

Jarron
surprise me

Dana
croissants, coffee, juice, cake

Jarron
sounds delicious

He grabs her.

She squeals.

They kiss for a moment.

Jarron
again

They kiss some more.

Dana
you're greedy

Jarron
of course

Dana
you'd think you'd never been kissed –

Jarron
not by you

Dana
you have to be quiet, I share this flat

Jarron
I don't care

Dana
actually, seriously

Jarron
you're quite hungry

Dana
finally he hears!

Jarron
you think I've had my time

Dana
shut up

Jarron
you're bored and want to get rid of me

Dana
never

Jarron
that's why you looked at the sun

Dana
the day has begun, that's all

Jarron
I'll pay you extra

Dana
what?

Jarron
I'll give you a bit more

Dana
a bit more what?

Jarron
money
you're a business woman, I know how this works

Dana
you think you are paying?

Jarron
aren't I?

Dana
what?

Jarron
what?

Dana
what?

Jarron
now wait a minute –

Dana
fucking cheek

Jarron
you came up to me, no introduction

Dana
I liked the look of you

Jarron
you liked the look of me?

Dana
is that so odd?
you said you worked for the UN, I was curious

Jarron
you were wearing practically nothing, underwear

Dana
it was a dress

Beat.

it was a dress

Jarron
that was a dress?

Dana
where do you come from?

Jarron
I've seen dresses but really –
I'm sorry. I made a mistake

Dana
too right you did
Christ alive. I can't believe you thought – Jesus

Jarron
girls don't come up to me like you did.

Dana
I'm not a girl
my name is Dana
I have a degree. I have a fucking mind which I can
make up.

Dana sits up with the sheet about her knees.

Jarron
so? I pay for sex, I thought everyone does

Dana
not around here

Jarron
they do where I come from

Dana
and where the fuck is that
hell?

He laughs.

Dana
don't laugh

Jarron
   well stop making jokes

Dana
   I'm serious
   sex that you pay for is toxic
   an irritant, feels nice for a second but

Jarron
   it suits me

Dana
   you don't know any other way, you've forgotten any
   other way

Jarron
   yeah, maybe I have

Dana
   then someone should show you

Beat.

   I would offer but you just offended me. Seriously
   offended

Jarron
   I said I was sorry

Beat.

He is tempted for a second.

Then he pulls away.

   you ought to wear more when you go out
   you ought to be more careful about the message you
   send

Dana
   everyone wears stuff like that

He starts to put his trousers on.

Dana
   where are you going?

Jarron
I've got miles to drive today
I have to get down to the Adriatic, over to North
Africa

Dana
and that's it?

Jarron
well, what else is there?

Dana
I made you an offer

Jarron
which you then retracted

Dana
OK, it's there. The offer.
I'll make love to you because I want to.
and you can make love to me, knowing that.

Beat.

Jarron
I don't have time

Dana
oh, it's scary –?

He looks at her.

Jarron
you don't know me

Dana
I didn't know you before

Jarron
we talked for an hour in the bar we got shitfaced we
screwed each other

Dana

we were tender we kissed

Jarron

stop it
fucking stop it

Dana

I can't believe this is so hard for you
it's two people, two consenting adults
don't worry you don't have to fall in love with me –

Jarron

I thought I knew what we were doing here
I thought we both knew what was going on, I thought
this was up and down, around and about, both parties
agreed all OK

Dana

it is OK

Jarron

no it's not fucking OK

Dana

of course it's OK

He reaches for his shirt.

Dana

you don't need to run quite so fast

Jarron

this doesn't happen to me.
I am a really powerful person, people don't trick me

Dana

I didn't trick you

Jarron

this is fucked up. This is really fucked up. I organise
people for a living, I write reports, I travel miles and

miles, people don't do this to me. I don't get caught
like this

Dana
you aren't caught

He does his buttons up.

Jarron
I don't drink with women in bars for real. You get it.

Dana
what is wrong with saying I like you, I think you're
nice

He puts his shoes on.

Jarron
nice? Do you want to know how not nice I am?
what if I tell you I only came with you because I could
see you had some goodness, I could see I could break
your heart

Dana
get over yourself
I came to you not the other way around

Jarron
I still ended up with my cock up your arse.

Beat.

I thought you would notice my semen is black, my
face twisting, my nails ridged, in short it didn't occur
to me you would do anything other than hold me in
contempt. I am unloveable, the unloved. Not the sort
of person that gets told they are nice. Feared maybe,
fucking hated, yes. I am a devil, I told you, a demon,
a thunderclap, I am a really fucking powerful person.
People cross the road to get out of my way, I am a
nightmare, an underpass in the dark, an alleyway, a
bridge that you don't cross.

Dana

I think I've got it.

Jarron

you fucking crazy bitch.

Dana

I didn't realise you were playing a game.
you should have said

Jarron

that would have ruined it.
fucking nice. You fucking load of shit.
don't give me nice

He has put his clothes on.

I've got to go. I've got a thousand miles to drive today.

Dana

you already said that

He starts to go.

He comes back.

Jarron

I really think I should pay you.
I just think this will be cleaner if I give you something
I slept here after all. I'll give you something for the bed

Dana

I don't want anything

Jarron

you must want something. There is always something.
a new phone or another dress. Get yourself another
dress –
why won't you take my money?

Dana

why does it bother you?

Jarron
  alright. Alright, I get it. You're not desperate
  you are not for sale
  you think love can't be bought, admirable but slightly
  outdated, but still. I admire that.

Beat.

  I don't want this to be left messy, like either of us have
  any reason to even think about last night ever again.
  I have important things to think about, I don't want to
  think about you

Dana
  so don't think about me then

Jarron
  you'll want money in the end.

Dana
  I doubt it

Jarron
  I'm a fucking demon I told you. A god. I want to play
  fucky fucky with your head, it's done.

Dana
  what does that mean?

Jarron
  two weeks and you'll be begging me to pay you.

Dana
  I don't think so

He picks up his jacket.

Jarron
  bye bye Dana

Dana
I'm not scared of you, yes you've got a trumped-up
ego, but you've got no power.
what power have you got?

He goes out of the door.

we fucking used a condom.
don't try and scare me.

Dana is left alone.

fucking cretin.

She kicks out at the sheets.

moron.
oh god.

THREE

Dana goes into a room where her sister is getting dressed.

Dana
I fucked a demon

Jasmine
you what?

Dana
I fucking fucked a demon.
all night long.

Jasmine
all night long?

Dana
yes
several times, lots of different ways. Oh shit, lots of
different ways

Her sister looks at her. Takes her in.

Goes back to brushing her hair.

Jasmine
well never mind

Dana
I'm being serious
he said he was from the UN

Jasmine
and was he?

Dana
I don't know

Jasmine
why do you do these things?

Dana
he looked nice. He stood at the end of the bar by the
window, I was carrying stuff past him, he moved out
of the way

Jasmine
you fucked him because he moved out of the way?

Dana
not just that, obviously, but it was a kind thing to do,
I was carrying all these bags and my laptop, there was
only a tiny space

Jasmine
are you completely desperate?

Dana
I thought maybe we would fall in love and live in each
other's arms
that was a joke by the way
I thought he might buy me a drink, light me a cigarette

Jasmine

for goodness sake

Dana

he could have tripped me up
he could have pushed me over, he could have spat in
my face

Jasmine

he could have done. Yes.
go and have a bath or something
forget him.

Dana stands at the window.

Dana

I tried that

Beat.

Jasmine

you're the one that is always telling me to move on,
flick a switch in your head and let him fall out the
back

Dana

and look what good that did you

Jasmine

I bet he didn't even leave his number.

Dana

he knows where I live, he might come back –
how far is the Adriatic?

Jasmine

the Adriatic?

Dana

that's where he is headed

Jasmine

Dana, stop this.

Dana
something happened between us

Beat.

I know how silly that sounds.

Beat.

Jasmine
aren't you supposed to be getting ready?

Dana
why?

Jasmine
hello

Dana
oh god

Jasmine
you hadn't forgotten?

Dana
what time is it?

Jasmine
ten to

Dana
shit

Jasmine
what has got into you?

Dana
I'll make it I'll make it
oh Christ

Jasmine
I'm not going to bring you coffee
I am not a waitress, a hand-maiden, I am not the

fucking mother, you forgot about it, OK. You can deal
with it

Dana starts to rush around looking for some clothes.

Dana
I can't believe this

Jasmine
where do you have to be anyway?

Dana
centre of town
where's my jacket?

Jasmine
I can't give you a lift either, I am not a taxi driver, a
chauffeur, you need a private secretary you get one
I'll ring you a taxi
my car's in the garage anyway so even if –

Dana
have you got a shirt I can borrow?

Jasmine
they're all creased

Dana
what about that one?

Jasmine
this one that I am wearing?

Dana
yes

Jasmine
this one I am wearing right now?

Dana
this is an emergency

Jasmine
    it's a grant interview
    let's be realistic

Dana
    for a grant I really want

Jasmine
    that you want so much you forgot the interview

Dana
    please can I borrow your shirt?
    I am your sister and I need some help

Jasmine
    a sister yes, but not a dependant
    unbelievable

Jasmine starts to take her shirt off.

So does Dana.

Jasmine
    have my skirt as well, why don't you?

Dana looks at it.

Dana
    no thanks

Jasmine
    fucking cheek
    I have a job as well you know

Dana
    oh heck, I was going to polish my shoes

Jasmine
    no time for that. Here.

Jasmine takes her shoes off and passes them to Dana.

Dana
    you don't need them today?

Jasmine
I'm not doing anything that is life-critical, no. anything else?

Dana
my brain to be in gear

Jasmine
you're on your own there –

Dana takes her shirt off.

Underneath she has a mark.

Dana
I can't believe after all this work I would nearly forget the damn thing

Jasmine
what's that?

Dana
where?

Jasmine
under your bra

Dana
nothing

She looks.

nothing

Jasmine
what sort of sex did you have?

Dana
well, what is it –

Jasmine comes over and looks at her.

Jasmine
looks like a hicky

Dana
   oh

Jasmine
   from a wolf
   who was this guy?

Dana goes and looks in the mirror.

Dana
   do you think it's possible to fall in love at first sight?

Jasmine
   oh fucking hell

Dana
   I didn't say I loved him, just

She looks at the mark.

   just a hicky

Jasmine
   exactly
   leave it alone then

Dana looks again.

Dana
   what time is it?

Jasmine
   five to.

Dana
   alright
   how do I look?

Jasmine
   not bad

Dana
   I actually think I should get some cream

Jasmine
  it's just a hicky

Dana
  I know

Jasmine
  please don't get a thing about a hicky, I know this man
  spooked you

Dana
  it's just a bit sore.
  You know how my skin reacts

Jasmine
  it probably wasn't even him.

Dana
  exactly
  it probably was there yesterday

Jasmine
  well there you are then.

Dana
  have you got some cream?

Jasmine
  get some on the way home

Dana
  what if he has done something to me?

Jasmine
  there are no demons, right.

Dana
  he said he was a god

Jasmine
  there are no gods.
  Dana, are you serious? A god. You believe in gods now?

Dana
his semen was black

Jasmine
then fucking wash yourself.
man's disgusting. Yuk.

Beat.

Dana
I will.
after my interview.
how do I look?

Jasmine
you'll knock them dead. You know that? You always do.

FOUR

Dana in her interview.

She sits on a chair, bathed in bright light.

The voices of several interviewers seem to come from all around her.

Interviewer 1
Miss Dana Edwards?

Dana
yes

Interviewer 2
thank you for coming, Miss Edwards

Dana
no problem

Interviewer 1
we would like to go over some aspects of your
application if you don't mind

Dana

of course

Interviewer 3

when you said you would like to set up a research group could you expound your area of expertise?

Dana

Customer Dynamics, which sounds rather dry but is actually a new and exciting theory on customer–business relationships that redefines interchange of information and transactions using psychoanalytical modelling and techniques, likening the customer–business contact to other basic human interactions, such as love.

Beat.

sorry, such as lust
such as friendship. I mean friendship, I don't know why I said that. Such as friendship, and if you were to apply the right indices to a variety of different forms of friendship after all –

Beat.

I'm sorry I seem to have lost my thread.
friendship, mutual outcomes working together, that is the essence of what commerce is trying to persuade the individual,
that the needs are mutual, when in fact of course they are different but –
I meant to say such as found in original bartering-type cultures. We find the roots of all financial transactions in . . .

She comes to a stop again.

do you mind if I look at my notes?

Interviewer 2
take your time

Dana looks at her notes.

She puts them the right way up.

She feels a bit hot.

Dana
the research I am doing is to try to pinpoint every
human interaction into the same framework

Interviewer 3
you already said that.

Dana
I know I said that.
could we turn this light down, only it's shining right
in my eyes

Interviewer 2
we don't have a lot of time, Miss Edwards, we have
quite a few candidates to see today, I am sure you
appreciate

Dana
of course

She feels like an idiot.

She goes back to her notes.

She re-starts.

customer exchanges occur over a wide range of
communication channels, and there is no distinction in
these channels between other communications that the
customer might receive. You might in the same second
get a text from your partner, and then from your bank.
To maximise the feeling of mutuality, should the text
from your bank feel *more* on your team than from

your partner? It is *your* bank, there to listen to you.
It may take a role and a flavour, a character if you like.
I think with the right modelling Customer Dynamics
could go beyond the transactional nature of the
interaction to look at emotions, intent and desires. If
we start to view each interaction as a chain of events
with a narrative –

Beat.

She has come to a full stop.

> oh, I see you are writing, I was wondering if you were
> still listening.

Interviewer 2
> we are just making some notes.

Dana
> I wondered if I had bored you

Interviewer 1
> sorry?

Dana
> I just meant –
> well it doesn't sound, I know it doesn't sound –
> the people out there are here to study Milton. And
> Dante and Goethe. They were telling me all this stuff
> about poetry, about our understanding of –
> well they can explain I didn't really get it but . . .
> I wish you would turn these lights down I can't really
> see you.

Interviewer 3
> have you any other questions, Miss Edwards?

Beat.

Dana
> sorry I didn't mean it is dull. I just meant, next to
> poetry. It's important to our understanding though, of

course, crucial and could add so much to the sales of an emerging business

Interviewer 1
thank you so much, Miss Edwards

Dana
I should have said that perhaps at the start. I think it's important.

Interviewer 2
thank you

Dana
what about the rest of my presentation?

Silence.

She gets off the chair.

OK
OK I see
shit.

FIVE

The library on the way home.

A Librarian, a tall gangly and deeply precise man, is stacking books on some shelves.

Dana
sorry. Can I speak to you?

Librarian
if you would like

Dana
I mean I won't disturb anyone

Librarian
this is a library, you have to be quiet

Dana
OK but I can talk?

Librarian
you can talk to me, you can't talk to your friends

Dana
that's OK, my friends aren't here. Just me.

She has tried to make a joke, it hasn't worked.

Beat.

I am looking for a book about demons

Librarian
we are about to close, I should warn you.

Dana
oh. Should I come back?

Librarian
what sort of demons?

Dana
I am not sure. I was wondering if there are pictures of demons in literature

Librarian
pictures in literature?

Dana
well pictures, obviously not pictures. Descriptions

Librarian
plenty.
where shall we start, Shakespeare, Proust?

Dana
Milton

Librarian
Milton?

Dana

does he have anything interesting to say about demons?

Librarian

Lots. Where do you want to start?

Dana

you tell me

Librarian

maybe you want to see our Milton specialist, they are in on a Wednesday, I can make you an appointment

Dana

I'm really only browsing.

Librarian

browsing for demon literature?

Dana

yes.

Librarian

you don't have time to browse, we are about to close

Dana

OK, what about Dante? Goethe?

Librarian

you can't just say Dante / Goethe.
Literature is like the universe, a solar system. Dante and Goethe are different planets. You can't dot about like this, picking names from anywhere. We have to start at the beginning. Era, context, meaning.

Dana

do you have any books that might help me?

Beat.

Librarian

what is your specific question?

Dana
my specific question?

Librarian
yes

Dana
alright
what happens if you piss one off?

Librarian
a demon?

Dana
yes
it's a hypothetical question

Librarian
I realise it is hypothetical, I am a librarian.

Dana
of course you are

Librarian
this is a library, the home of the hypothetical question

Dana
exactly

Librarian
have you pissed one off?

Dana
of course not.

Dana laughs.

The Librarian laughs.

Dana laughs again.

Dana
yes

Librarian
very funny

Dana
what would happen?

Librarian
a god or a demon?

Dana
both, either

Librarian
so something powerful?

Dana
yes

Librarian
that you pissed off?

Dana
yes

Librarian
lightning would strike I guess

Dana
in literature?

Librarian
in literature

Dana
can you be a bit more specific?

Librarian
can you?

Dana
alright, say the demon thinks he owes you a debt, but you didn't let him pay

Librarian
a demon wouldn't get into debt

Dana
well, say he did

Librarian
how could he?

Dana
just hypothetically say it had happened

Librarian
but we are talking about literature here, right?
we are taking our examples from literature,
so we only have the examples that other people have
written. It isn't like a phrase book

Dana
OK, I just thought there might be some guidance.
don't you think they are out there, they might be an
owner of a business or someone who robs you in the
street, or a father who is abusing someone

Librarian
it's a bit different

Dana
every age must have their equivalents.

Librarian
I only really know about literature
and –

Dana
the library is about to close

Librarian
exactly

Dana
I was just asking what literature said of pissing off
someone like that –

Librarian

in literature someone who classed himself as a demon
wouldn't like to have a debt. He will work really hard
to make sure he doesn't owe anyone anything. That is
the basis of selling your soul. Devil or demon, they are
the original transactional creature.

Dana

so if he did think he owed you something?

Librarian

he wouldn't
he would find a way to pay it

Dana

you seem very absolute about that?

Librarian

I don't know all of literature, I am mainly a classicist

Dana

I understand but what about a mark? Might they leave
some sort of IOU on you?

Librarian

like what?

Dana

I am talking hypothetically

Librarian

of course you are

Dana

because we're in a library
what if a demon were to leave a sort of a sore –

Librarian

on your body?

Dana

yes.

Librarian
I would have to look that up.

Dana
well could you look it up?

Librarian
now?

Dana
yes please

Librarian
I could but we are about to close.

Beat.

I could look it up in the morning but tomorrow is my day off. I could look it up on Tuesday if you like.

Dana
OK

Librarian
but if a demon left a sore on my body, I wouldn't like it. The mark of the devil, well it's not going to be good, is it?

Dana
isn't it?

Librarian
I wouldn't have thought so, no.

Dana
hypothetically

Librarian
hypothetically of course.

SIX

Dana

OK you've had your fun. Very funny. Fucking demon
I am talking to you. You want to scare me. You want
to get in my head – too bad. I can put cream on the
mark. You've infected me with something I'll take a
tablet. Bring it on, you want to send me your curses,
I'll bat them back. I am invincible, stronger than you,
surrounded with a shield, a force of my own. I will
knock you sideways. I will bowl you over, I will wrap
you in a knot and tie you in ribbons. What do you
think of that? Hey, nightmare, a dark alleyway, a man
with a knife, a pain that won't stop, a roaring fire, a
child's face howling, hunger, plague, disease
I'm not scared of you
I am not scared of anyone, and particularly not you.
you get in my head, I'll leave you there
you get in my body, I will caress you
you get in my hair I will curl it and put it up

Jarron appears sitting at a table having a beer.

Jarron

you want a drink?

Dana

where were you?

Jarron

I had some work to do. I came back, didn't I?

Dana

you came back here?

Jarron

I drove to the south, I did my work, I came back

Dana
why?

Jarron
we hadn't finished

Dana
hadn't we?

Jarron
no we hadn't and I didn't like it
this needs to be over and done with now. And quickly.

Dana
quickly?

Jarron
I'm presuming you would have changed your mind

Dana
about what?

Jarron
the cheque. I have written it out, and before you ask
no it's not sizeable.

Dana
oh that

Jarron
it's 45 euros which I think is an adequate
representation of the time taking into account the
distress you have caused me, the inconvenience of
having to return. I have charted it all, put my petrol in,
my time, the wear and tear on my car, and 45 euros
left to you covers it I think.

Dana
is that right?

Jarron
if you want to make a different representation then we
can enter into a negotiation at the end of this meeting

Dana

this is a meeting?

Jarron

I am prepared to raise it slightly but only just. And before you say there is no debt, there is a debt. There is a big fucking debt, that is the only explanation

Dana

for what?

Jarron

for what has been happening with me since I saw you.
this sensation I have
this uncomfortable sensation,
why I can't control my thoughts as I should –
you are nothing, you are inconsequential, you aren't even beautiful.
you don't make me laugh. Your dress sense is terrible. Your teeth are crooked, your breath smells in the morning, you are ugly in some lights, not as clever as you think –

Dana

glad we've got that clear

Jarron

and you are a woman. Basically
you are a woman.
you aren't even nearly the sort of person I should be thinking about.

Beat.

please take the money and release me.
I thought I knew every trick in the book, but there is obviously one that got away.

Dana

I can't release you

Jarron
I'll pay you to undo it, how about that? 45 euros, it's
not a payment for the other night, it's a payment for
your unlocking services

Dana
and if I can't?

Jarron
find a way.

Dana
you want me to stop you from loving me?

Jarron
who talked about love?

Dana
that's the sensation you described

Jarron
it's not love

Dana
what is it?

Jarron
a curse of some kind.
you've made me obsessed by you

Dana
so you are obsessed?

Jarron
you fucking bitch, you don't have to smile

Beat.

this, this is over
you know that?

Dana
OK by me

Jarron
  things could get bad for you

Dana
  bring it on

Jarron
  why aren't you scared of me?

Dana
  because you aren't scary.
  you say you had your soul ripped out, but I can feel it
  still beating in the palm of my hand.

Jarron
  you'll take my money. In the end.

Dana
  what, and then you think you'll be free of me?

Jarron
  I'll forget you then, yes
  yes

Dana
  maybe

Jarron
  no good will come of this, you know that?

Dana
  we'll see

SEVEN

Dana is at home.

Jasmine
  Dana?
  Dana? You were talking to yourself

Dana

was I?

Jasmine

how did it go?

Dana

badly.
actually.

Jasmine

really?

Dana

yes, really badly.
I fucked up
I thought I was prepared and then, Jesus why wasn't
I better prepared?

Jasmine

you were prepared –

Dana

I got in there, and all the stuff I had meant to say

Jasmine

why do you always do this?

Dana

do what?

Jasmine

say it's all dreadful, a disaster and make me believe
you have failed, and then –

Dana

not this time

Jasmine

they rang for fuck's sake.
when they got me they left a message. You impressed

them, you impressed them very much. You impressed
them so much they are putting you forward for an
international position

Dana
an international position?

Jasmine
they want you to go and talk to their colleagues in
Alexandria

Dana
what?

Jasmine
some sort of cross-university team

Dana
in Alexandria?

Jasmine
they said ring them in the morning

Dana
there must be a mistake

Jasmine
you bloody aced it

Dana
did they actually use my name, maybe they rang the
wrong candidate?

Jasmine
they're putting you forward for an international award
for Christ's sake
forget Berlin

Dana
they'll ring in the morning and say there's been an
error –

Jasmine
will you stop for once?
you got it. Hello?
you got it with bells on, you're going to fucking
Alexandria

Beat.

Dana
I don't understand it

Jasmine
what is there to understand?

Dana
then the other candidates must have been really poor
or stupid,
I promise you I fucked up

Jasmine
for God's sake –

Dana
why are you cross with me?

Jasmine
when I fuck up, I really fuck up. That's the difference.
When you fuck up, you still win.

Dana
how was your day?

Jasmine
no worse than normal.

Dana looks at her.

and I'll miss you like hell if you move to Alexandria

Dana
I haven't got it yet. Have I?
they just want me to talk to the people in Alexandria

Jasmine
you'll get it. Why wouldn't you?

Dana
maybe I don't even want it.
when do they want me there?

Jasmine
Monday

Dana
this Monday?

Jasmine
better start packing.

Beat.

Dana
we were going to do something together this weekend

Jasmine
doesn't matter

Dana
look at some flats, see about our deposit

Jasmine
we've got lots of weekends

Dana
not if I go to Alexandria

Jasmine
I can amuse myself for forty-eight hours, don't worry

Dana
can you?

Jasmine
I'm not completely useless, I've got work to do

Dana
I'll lock the fridge

Jasmine

    I'm through that. Please.

    I'm through that.

Beat.

Dana

    I can't go to Alexandria for Monday

Jasmine

    course you can

Dana

    why don't you come too?

Jasmine

    I've got so much to catch up on

Dana

    bring it with you

    have a few days away

    we could get a train, see some of the coast

Jasmine

    which coast?

Dana

    I don't know, maybe the Adriatic

    take a boat

Jasmine

    why would we go to the Adriatic?

Dana

    I am just talking about making it more of a trip

    we always said we wanted to see more of Europe,

    the sea

    I was just thinking of ways to make it

Jasmine

    what?

Dana
more fun

Jasmine
by going a thousand miles out of our way?

Dana
isn't that the basis of an adventure?

Beat.

Jasmine
he's a dick, you know that

Dana
who?

Jasmine
the man you were with. All men are dicks but he is a high-class representative of his species. Even Jerome said he was a dick and that is saying something

Dana
I wasn't talking about him

Jasmine
you told me he was headed for the Adriatic

Dana
did I?

Jasmine
and he's some kind of con man.
seriously, he is fucking dangerous. I went into the bar this morning, he didn't pay for all his drinks, tried to con the waitress, then left a credit card number that didn't work.

Dana
why are you telling me this?

Jasmine
because I think you're still thinking about him

Dana

that's ridiculous. Even if he was at the Adriatic, that
isn't an address, there must be a million people there

Jasmine

so that isn't why you would go that way?

Dana

absolutely not
the Adriatic is beautiful I've heard, and –
he was a passing moment. One night of something,
but in the cold light of day meaningless
and I don't want to see him again.
I can't see him again
how could I see him again?
thank god for you setting me right. Men like that, who
needs them?

Jasmine

maybe I should come with you –

Dana

you don't have to

Jasmine

a couple of days away

Dana

you'd be bored

Jasmine

keep you company

Dana

there are a million people in the Adriatic, how could
I find him?

Jasmine

it won't stop you trying
he works for the UN, that is a start

Dana
I'll be fine

Jasmine
I know, but as you say it's ages since I have been on a trip.

Dana
really?

Jasmine
you think you are the only person that can behave rashly?

Dana
we only have one suitcase

Jasmine
we can share
we share everything else.

Dana
it's a bit fucking hasty

Jasmine
and you aren't?

Jasmine goes and gets the suitcase.

She puts it out in front of Dana.

Beat.

Dana
I don't have to take a job thousands of miles away

Jasmine
you might want to

Dana
I'll just go to see

Jasmine
  you can't live with your sister for ever
  even I know that, this is a phase that one day will end

Dana
  I like living with you

Jasmine
  I tie you down

Dana
  not at all.

Beat.

Jasmine
  alright, you tie me down then

Dana
  fuck off.

Jasmine
  I'd be OK you know. Without you.

Dana
  of course you would.

Beat.

Jasmine
  why are you looking at me like that?

Dana
  I'm not

Jasmine
  I'm not a charity case, OK after Mum and Dad died,
  but –

Dana
  I know what is going on

Jasmine
how can you know?

Dana
I've guessed

Beat.

Jasmine
you guessed?

Dana
tell me I'm wrong.

Jasmine
if you've guessed why the hell didn't you say?

Dana
I was waiting for you to say something.

Jasmine
and what if I didn't?

Dana
you'd have to eventually

Jasmine
does it show?

Dana
only on your face.

Beat.

Jasmine
it shows on my face?

Dana
a bit.

Jasmine
alright. So you're the clever one. So tell me, what am I going to do? I'm on my own.

Dana

you're going to pack a bag and come with me to
Alexandria, and we'll have the whole train journey to
work that out.

Jasmine

I thought you'd be angry, I thought you'd stomp about
and say how could I have been so stupid. I'm supposed
to be a grown-up –

Dana

well, how could you have been stupid?

Jasmine

I don't know. I have no fucking idea
well, I have some idea but in specifics, no, fuck knows

Dana

fuck did know

Jasmine

yes, fuck did know

Dana

was it Jerome?

Jasmine

I don't want to talk about who it was

Dana

Jerome

Jasmine

Dana –

Dana

pack your bag

Jasmine

are you sure?

Dana

two women and an unborn baby going to Alexandria.
What could be better?

Jasmine smiles.

Jasmine
I am not a fucking sob story though. Promise me, this isn't a poor Jasmine thing?

Dana
no, it's a poor fucking Dana thing, I've got to put up with you. Puking, no – mood swings – give me strength.

EIGHT

Dana is back in the library.

The Librarian is there.

Dana
I wondered have you got any of those books that I ordered –

Librarian
we aren't open quite

Dana
it's nine o'clock

Librarian
not by my watch. It's a minute to

Dana
I have a train to catch –

Librarian
this is a council library. We have to do things the council's way

Dana
and that is?

Librarian
at the appointed time

Dana
  my watch says nine

Librarian
  it's my watch that counts
  and the clock on the wall, the library clock

Dana
  alright, but maybe I could just talk to you while –

Librarian
  fifty-one, fifty-two
  you see the second hand

Dana
  I don't want to miss my train

Librarian
  fifty-seven, fifty-eight. Fifty-nine
  can I help you?

Dana
  I came in before.

Librarian
  oh yes
  about the mark

Dana
  not just the mark

Librarian
  the demon I remember, you –
  you ordered every book in the entire city's collection
  on devils, marks, sexually transmitted marks, whether
  they have AIDS in hell, they haven't come in yet, sorry

Dana
  what?

Librarian
  you overloaded the system, it will be a day or two

Dana
I can't wait a day or two

Librarian
well next time just order one book not nine hundred

Dana
you are sure there is nothing?

Librarian
there is one thing

Dana
yes

Librarian
it appears we overcharged you
there's a small note on your file

Dana
that can't be right –

Librarian
you had a few fines a couple of years back, and it says
here that you paid them, but going through it looks
like we owe you a rebate

Dana
a rebate? I've never been in the library before

Librarian
says here

Dana
must be a mistake

Librarian
45 euros is the number that is coming up.
I can pay you now if you like

Dana
oh I see

Librarian
I could write a cheque or just give you the cash

Dana
I knew it was you

Librarian
I'm sorry

Dana
of course you would keep trying. I should have thought.
put it away I told you I won't take it

Librarian
alright, we could do a bank transfer

Dana
I know this is a test, you can test me all you want, I won't fail,
overcharged me for a non-existent library fine, you'll have to do better than that

Librarian
excuse me

Dana
I'm no fool, I am on to you and your tricks
devil

Librarian
listen, lady

Dana
black semen ridged nails

Librarian
now wait a minute

Dana
scar on your chest where they tore your soul out

Dana pushes him.

Librarian
I would rather you didn't do that

Dana
stop it, you stop it right now
stop pretending

She grabs him.

Librarian
would you mind taking your hands off me?

Dana
not until you admit it's you

Librarian
admit I'm who?

They fight.

She rips his shirt.

He is pushed over on the library floor.

Dana
no scar?

Librarian
who on earth do you think you are?

Dana
you aren't him?

Librarian
who? The demon?

Dana
sorry

Librarian
you thought I was the demon?

Dana
I mistook you

Librarian
I was actually trying to help you
I was trying to be nice
the council doesn't often hand out rebates.
you should be so blessed.

He gets up.

insanity. The first symptom of possession.

Dana
I am not insane

Librarian
thinks they have a mark

Dana
I have a mark

Librarian
it's in your mind

Dana
what is this then?

She lifts up her T-shirt.

Librarian
that's it?

Dana
yes

Librarian
it looks like a mosquito bite

Dana
it hurts

She covers herself up with her shirt.

it hurts a lot
and it's getting bigger.

Librarian
I suggest cream then.

Dana
brilliant

Librarian
antiseptic cream.

Dana
I could have thought of that myself, how helpful

Librarian
helpfulness, that's what I am here for.

Dana starts to go.

you know I once fucked a demon

Dana
excuse me?

Librarian
don't think that you are the only person that has taken
that road. Uncomfortable and gorgeous all at the same?
regrettable and delicious. It was many moons ago, but
I remember it well.
run run, you've got a train to catch.

NINE

Dana and Jasmine are on the train.

Dana
I just think it's a general principle, you shouldn't let
people give you money. Even the council. Not unless
you want it. Not unless you ask for it. I hadn't asked
for it. In fact I had specifically said

Jasmine
this is a general principle?

Dana

we don't know who he was, he said he was a librarian. He worked in a library, so what? He could have been anyone

Jasmine

well, we know who he wasn't

Dana

men in particular. I don't think we should be taking money from men, and keep your guard, Jasmine, don't let people push money into your hand saying it is for me.

Jasmine

it's like you are at war

Dana

I am

Jasmine

over what?

Beat.

you know there is no such thing as a demon, right?

Dana

yes

Jasmine

glad we've got that clear

Beat.

Dana

but if there was such a thing, it would be just like him to change his appearance and become other people. You said he was a con man –

Jasmine

I can't do this. I can't go on a trip with you if you are going mad.

I am the one that has hormones rushing through my body. If anyone is entitled to go mad it is me.

Dana
go mad then.

Beat.

Jasmine
I did go mad. I came with you

Dana laughs a bit.

oh, you can still laugh?

Jasmine laughs a bit.

Dana laughs a lot.

Jasmine
there's supposed to be a nice bar on the main square and we've got an hour at Budapest station

Dana
sounds good

Jasmine
get a bloody great bottle of wine –

Dana
you shouldn't be drinking

Jasmine
I haven't decided anything yet

Dana
we'll buy a bottle and I'll end up drinking it all

Jasmine
and?

Dana
I have to give a presentation on Monday
I have to be sharp, together

Jasmine
you're going to end up a professor, aren't you?
you're going to end up one of those really smart
people that has written lots of books

Dana
I still won't earn as much as you –

Jasmine
I don't earn a lot. I earn a normal amount.

The Train Inspector comes along.

Inspector
there is actually a problem with your card

Dana
what sort of problem?

Inspector
the card you used to buy the tickets with, the bank's
refused it.

Dana
that's impossible

Inspector
you'll either have to get off at the next station or pay
again

Dana
are you serious?

Inspector
that's the rules, I'm sorry to say

Jasmine
wait a minute, could you try the card again?

Inspector
if it's already been refused –

Jasmine
sometimes the phone lines get twisted, try again

The Inspector takes Dana's card.

The machine doesn't seem to like it.

Jasmine
are you using the right PIN?

Dana
don't be a moron

Dana punches in her PIN.

It doesn't work.

She takes the card out.

She kind of waves it around for a second.

She puts it back in.

Jasmine
try mine

She gets her card out.

Inspector
thank you

The Train Inspector puts the card in.

He hands the card machine to Jasmine.

Jasmine puts her PIN number in.

The card comes back out.

Jasmine
now that is ridiculous

Dana
it has to be your machine

Inspector
don't worry, you can get off at the next station and
ring your bank

Dana

we can't get off at the next station

Jasmine

we are trying to get to Athens then across to
Alexandria

Inspector

you're travelling without a ticket
that's an offence, sorry to say

Dana

how much cash have you got, maybe we could get
singles

Jasmine

I haven't got much cash on me

Inspector

two singles to Budapest, 90 euros

Dana

how much have you got, Jasmine?

Jasmine

I'm just looking
sixteen, eighteen

Dana

I've got another ten

Jasmine

thirty-six, I didn't think we'd need it

Dana

it's not enough.

Jasmine

is there someone we could phone?

Inspector

sometimes there are some deals
see what you can get to

She looks in her purse again.

Jasmine
    I might have, yes another five
    forty-one

Inspector
    if you could make it to 45, you could have a two-for-
    one offer

Jasmine
    sounds good, another three –

Dana
    what two-for-one offer?

Inspector
    technically not official till next month, but I can bend
    the rules a little

Dana
    you'd give us a free ticket?

Inspector
    they're only singles and you'd have to sort yourself out
    when you change at Budapest, but –

Dana
    sorry we can't take them

Jasmine
    what?

Dana
    we aren't taking his made-up offer
    I know what this is

Jasmine
    Dana, you are really fucking crazy, do you know that

Dana
    I told you, we don't take money

Jasmine
it isn't money

Dana
it's 45 euros

Jasmine
it isn't actual cash

Inspector
only do you want it?

Dana
no

Jasmine
yes
excuse me.
I can't do this, I can't do this.

Dana
you do what you want, I'm not taking his money

Jasmine
it's not his money

Dana
you go on then, I'll get off, sort the bank and meet you
in Budapest

Jasmine
what, you would leave me?

Dana
it's a city, you'd be fine in a city. No fridges

Jasmine
fuck off

Inspector
I am sorry I am going to have to ask you to leave
the train

either that or I will have to phone the police to escort
you

Dana
fine, I've got it

Jasmine
Dana
I'm sorry about this

Inspector
only there's the rest of the train I need to see to

Jasmine
can you give me one ticket to Budapest please?

Dana
you'd leave me?

Jasmine
you've gone mad
yes I would.

The Inspector gives Jasmine a ticket.

The Inspector goes.

Dana and Jasmine look at each other.

Jasmine is flicking her ticket.

Dana
where the hell is the next place anyway?

Jasmine
Hartenharten

Dana
Hartenharten, that's a place?

Jasmine
shit happens, Dana, why does your life have to be so
elaborate, so fucking dramatic? It is all some conspiracy,

some ordained way of putting you in the centre of the
universe. Our cards got refused, so what?

Beat.

Dana
you don't get it

Jasmine
damn right I don't.

Beat.

so will I meet you in Budapest or not?

Dana
don't look at me like that

Jasmine
did you use a condom?

Dana
of course I did.

Jasmine
for every hole?

Beat.

stupid cow

Dana
you don't go mad from an STD

Jasmine
oh, so you admit you are mad now.
what is black semen anyway, some kind of blood
thing?

Dana
I don't know

Jasmine
did you actually see his semen, or did he just tell you
that?

78

Dana

do we have to talk about this so loudly?
everybody already is looking

Jasmine

how is the hicky?

Dana

I know, how about a loudhailer?
it grew into a boil then it burst yellow pus

Jasmine

are you serious?

Dana

I'm joking.
of course it didn't

Jasmine

oh, excuse me for saying anything, you just screwed a
man with black semen that you think is a devil –

Dana

it got quite big, I put cream on it

Jasmine

glad to see you can see the humour in this.
that's the station. By the way.
your stop.

Dana

what?

Jasmine

Hartenharten

Dana

where the hell is that even?

Jasmine

it's here.

Dana
OK, I'll meet you tonight.
Budapest station.

Jasmine
well what time?

Dana
as soon as I can. I'll ring you.
I'll be on the next train

She picks up the suitcase.

who takes the suitcase?

Jasmine
don't be so fucking stupid, you know I'll come with you.
you drive me crazy you know that?

TEN

Dana is giving part of her presentation.

Dana
I thought I would take a recent example. Customer
transactions. I am going to subtitle this section of my
presentation, 'How to still be civil when something
goes wrong'. You see just a day or so ago, I was on a
train and there was something wrong with my card.
Now the usual situation is that in the inspector's mind
the customer quickly changes from a would-be positive
collaborator on our shared enterprise of paying and
experiencing a pleasant-as-advertised journey to some
kind of criminal, eager to see the company diddled,
whereas in the customer's mind they are still simply
trying to pay. But in this instance, this sort of
interaction – the rules appeared to shift –

The Librarian taps her on the shoulder.

Librarian

I have those books you ordered

Dana

what are you doing here?

Librarian

I'm in Hartenharten for the weekend
I work in Hartenharten on the weekends
we have a pretty good library, and as you see it's open.

Dana

I didn't know there was a library

Librarian

you have brought yourself here
you walked right in the door
the rest of Hartenharten shuts at five, but we are open
more or less all the time

Dana

you live in Berlin. I saw you in Berlin only this morning

Librarian

this is like my other job, and look some of your books
are on these shelves, so we might as well –

Dana

are you following me?

Librarian

why would I follow you?
listen, don't knock it, I'm trying to help you. Last time
I just about got pulverised for it, luckily I am resilient.
And ever-helpful. The true librarian to the end. If you
don't want these books I can just put them back on the
shelves for you, or you can fill out a little yellow slip
for reserved.

Dana

OK I'll take them

The Librarian passes Dana a couple of books.

Librarian

first things first, a guidebook to Hartenharten,

Dana

I didn't ask for that

Librarian

maybe not, but I put in a few extras and believe me
you'll need it. The illustrations are very good although
it comes to the conclusion of many, don't stay here
long. My advice pretty much concurs with that for
what it's worth, get back on a main-route train as fast
as you can. My second suggestion is a 'how to' book.
Always the best, you can't go wrong with a 'how to'
book. This one, *How to Live with No Money*,
published a few years ago but still one of the classics.

Dana

what do you mean, no money?

Librarian

I mean not much money.

Dana

we have lots of money

Librarian

look, do you want these books or not?

Dana

we have lots of money in our bank account
we just need a bank

Librarian

third, *How to Survive an Economic Disaster*. Bit
outdated, but –

Dana

if you could just tell me where the bank is

Librarian

fourth book. *How to Find a Bank when They Have All Shut*

Dana

why have they shut?

Librarian

do you read the papers? Watch the news?

Dana

what has happened?

Librarian

it was on the cards for a while, if you care to read Jefferson's *Economic Reality in Post-euro Europe* you would have had it all predicted. Or Fresherman's *How the Early Twenty-first-Century Economists Got it All Wrong*
the banks have shut their doors
internal collapse, one after the other
just like before. Only they have done it again

Dana

they were fine yesterday

Librarian

they were teetering yesterday. They weren't fine yesterday. If you read the small print, the detail of what was going on
look do you want these books or not?

Dana takes the books.

Librarian

don't bother to thank me

Dana

thank you.

She looks at the books. There are quite a few.

will the bank be open tomorrow?

Librarian
unlikely, did you hear what I said?

Dana
so, what? Is there a hotel we can stay in for the night?

Librarian
out the library, turn left. Metropole Street. Probably listed in the guidebook under places to particularly avoid but there isn't another one. Don't eat the breakfast, sleep with the lights on. Don't use the bath unless you are carrying disinfectant with you.

Dana
why are you looking after me?

Librarian
I'm not.
I'm looking after me.

Dana
where am I headed?

Librarian
don't ask.

ELEVEN

The hotel in Hartenharten.

Dana and Jasmine stand in their hotel room with their suitcase.

Jasmine
I knew we should have got a plane.

Beat.

Dana
it's not bad

Jasmine
it's not good

Dana
it's a bit cold.

Jasmine
it's fucking freezing.
one night?

Dana
yes
one night

Jasmine
it's so cold I can feel my bones

Dana
there must be some heating.

Jasmine
the windows don't even shut

Dana
we'll stuff them with clothes.

Beat.

it's just one night.

Jasmine
I know

Dana
I agree it's not great, is that a heater?

Jasmine
I think it was.

Dana
sit down I'll put the kettle on.

Jasmine sits down.

Jasmine
    you know I'm crap at the cold

Dana
    you'll be fine

Jasmine
    there is cold and there is cold.
    what if we wake up and we are frozen?

Dana
    you've got the baby to keep you warm

Jasmine
    poor ice-covered little thing

Dana
    maybe you should stay with the suitcase and I'll go
    and look for the bank

Jasmine
    you just looked for a bank

Dana
    well there must be another bank.
    OK so one shut their doors but there must be another
    one.
    they are all connected.

Jasmine
    I live in the real world, Dana. They shut their doors
    they shut their doors. I thought it wasn't supposed to
    happen again.

Beat.

Dana
    tea?

Jasmine
    yes please.

Dana starts the kettle.

Dana

that will warm you up.
oh fuck, the kettle doesn't work

Jasmine

Jesus.

Beat.

no one loses all their money overnight, do they?

Dana

I guess not

Jasmine

there are regulations for this kind of thing, when
banks close, people are OK?

Dana

yes or they have been in the past

Jasmine

exactly everyone was OK last time, weren't they? The
countries were screwed but the individuals were OK.

Dana

I guess so

Jasmine

so we'll be fine then –

Dana

I need to get to Alexandria for Monday

Jasmine

so there are the big things like whether we have just
been bankrupted and then there are the small things
like whether we can get to Alexandria for Monday

Dana

it isn't a small thing

Jasmine

no but it isn't like losing all one's savings.

Dana
you've got the car

Jasmine
yes if we can get home, I've got the car.

Dana
I need to get to Alexandria, without this grant –

Jasmine
you'll get to Alexandria
we have what, forty-eight hours, we could walk if we
have to.

Dana
hardly

Jasmine
it's a setback, yes.
we are temporarily suspended.
do you think we are going to actually be able to sleep
here?
I mean I don't want to be fussy but
oh fucking hell

Beat.

She takes a deep breath.

what we need is an embassy. We're Europeans. We'll
go to the embassy tomorrow and tell them what has
happened, OK? This sort of thing happens, all the
time. No one actually loses money. They sort it

Dana
and in the meantime?

Jasmine
there is no meantime, this will be sorted.
bit of a pisser that we have to stay here tonight, but
basically –

Dana
what will we eat?

Jasmine
what?

Dana
aren't you hungry?
we haven't eaten anything since lunch

Jasmine
do you have to always turn to the problems?

Dana
we need to eat something don't we?
you are pregnant

Jasmine
and we will eat, we'll eat food

Dana
you spent all our euros on that stupid ticket, and we
haven't even paid for this room –

Jasmine
when we go to the embassy we will explain we need
some petty cash to tide us over. We won't be the only
people in this boat. I told you.

Dana
there isn't an embassy

Jasmine
there'll be one in the next town

Dana
that's quite a walk

Jasmine
we'll ring ahead. Make an appointment, then when we
get there they'll give us a temporary chequebook or
something. A small amount of money. We'll go to the
top of the queue because of the baby

Dana

    I've got the bread from lunch

Jasmine

    there you are then
    we're fine

Dana

    tomorrow is a Saturday
    the embassy won't be open on a Saturday
    and the next day is Sunday

Jasmine

    we'll go Monday

Dana

    I have to be in Alexandria on Monday

Jasmine

    well, maybe in an emergency they will open the
    embassy even on a Saturday. I think this is an
    emergency, don't you? All the major banks in Europe
    folding at once.
    there'll be a number. An information sheet.
    someone will be printing up an information sheet and
    delivering them to all the hotels right now.

Dana

    OK.

Jasmine

    even in Hartenharten
    the information sheets will get through.

Beat.

    have you got any other food? Other than the bread?

Dana

    for tomorrow?

Jasmine

    not specifically for tomorrow, I just wanted to know

Dana
I feel a bit hungry now

Jasmine
that's the panic
you can't panic in a situation like this

Dana
what if we get really hungry in the night and we want
to eat all the food?

Jasmine
I'm through that, I told you

Dana
you're pregnant, anything could happen

Jasmine
don't turn this into I am the one who is fucking it up

Dana
OK calm down

Jasmine
if one of us wakes up in the night and eats all the food
it will be a bit of a bugger, but not a disaster because
we are both well-nourished and even a pregnant
woman can walk to the embassy in the next town with
no breakfast.

Dana
OK

Jasmine
OK
what else have you got?

Dana
not much
couple of bananas I think
some emergency contraception
some chocolate

Jasmine

there you are then – riches. I bet you could live on a packet of wine gums for a week if you had to.

Dana gets it out.

Dana

why are you so calm?

Jasmine

because we live in Europe, because nothing really bad happens. We both have jobs, the worst of this is, is a bit of an inconvenience and perhaps not such a good mini-break but really in the grand scheme of life, not so bad.

Dana

my phone is about to run out of charge

Jasmine

so charge it

Dana

I forgot the charger

Jasmine

what?

Dana

well, we packed in a hurry. If we had a week to make lists and think about the sort of things we might need it's normally you that remembers things like a charger

Jasmine

alright, when we get things sorted out, we'll get a charger

Dana

perfect

Jasmine

we have plenty of money after all. All our inheritance plus savings.

this is just a temporary situation.
you are the one that knows about customer relations.
There will be a number to call, won't there?

Dana
probably.

Jasmine
some way that the bank will have of smoothing this
over

Dana
if the bank is bust, technically it won't be the bank

Jasmine
alright, whoever's job it is to make this OK. They will
make it smooth.

Dana
that fucking demon

Jasmine
I'm tired
I'm so fucking tired. Please.
we've been travelling all day

Beat.

Dana
you're tired of me

Jasmine
I'm tired of this.
I'm tired generally, but yes, I am tired of you.
do you mind if I go to sleep?

Dana
I'm sorry

Jasmine
aren't you tired?
I know the beds are crap and the room like the Arctic
but

Dana
I'm not pregnant

Jasmine
lucky you.

Jasmine starts to go to sleep.

Dana stays up.

She turns down the light.

Dana
goodnight.
I love you.

Jasmine
love you too.

Dana
I'm sorry

Jasmine
don't be sorry, it's a fucking adventure.
we'll laugh one day.

Dana
very funny

Jasmine
we will.
when this child is born, we'll tell it about this hideous
place we came to on the way to Alexandria

Dana
when this child is born?

Jasmine
yes, right before you got the most amazing job

Dana
and right before you and the baby came out with me
to live in Alexandria,

Jasmine

and right before we got this really nice flat because you
became a professor, and we'll tell the baby, that life
was pretty OK but we did have to spend one night in a
fridge.

Dana

it will laugh and ask how can you live in a fridge when
a fridge is so small

Jasmine

ah, OK, we'll go not literally a fridge but a room that
was so cold you could see the ice forming

Dana

you should have been a poet

Jasmine

fuck off I'm going to sleep

Dana

that sounds nice by the way

Jasmine

what does?

Dana

talking to your baby.
when it's born

Jasmine

goodnight.

Dana

goodnight.

Dana looks around.

She opens her shirt and looks at the hicky.

She puts her hand up to it, it's sore to touch now.

All over her breast.

She turns round, it's all over her back too.

She takes a scrubbing brush to it.

TWELVE

Dana is in the bath.

The water is cold, but she doesn't notice.

In the bath with her is the demon.

He is sitting behind her and scrubbing her back.

Dana
surprise surprise

Jarron
what does that mean?

Dana
I knew you wouldn't stay away

Jarron
you're imagining me

Dana
whatever you say

Jarron
I'm a version in your head

Dana
OK by me.

Jarron
a weird version as it turns out
not quite me at full force
I would never get into a bath with a girl

He gets out of the bath and starts drying himself with a towel.

Jarron
what do you want?

Dana
I don't want anything

Jarron
so why am I here?

Dana
you brought yourself

Jarron
in your dreams

Dana
alright, I want to know why you are doing this?
I mean I know what you are trying to do, I just want
you to say it

Jarron
you think I did this?

Dana
didn't you?

Jarron
what does your sister say?

Dana
she didn't meet you

Jarron
just take the damn thing, then it wouldn't really matter
what the banks were doing, you could get to where
you need to go

Dana
we've been through this.

Jarron
a nice 45-euro-worth hamper of food

Dana

no thank you

Jarron

think of your sister
pregnant after all. That poor little baby

Dana

my sister has nothing to do with it

Jarron

and freezing cold
how about a radiator, or a hot-water bottle to put at
her feet?

Dana

this is between you and me
you keep her out of it

Jarron

I am a demon, I don't have any morals, any
boundaries. I can go sideways I can go up I can go
down. I can punish your great-granddaughter for this,
or your aged ancestor.
it's all a bit silly isn't it, for a principle? For pride?
for your ego, for putting yourself first.
you can name your price, if crisp banknotes aren't
your thing
two return tickets to Alexandria

Dana

we'll get to Alexandria

Jarron

you need that job
Berlin is more or less collapsing
Europe is in the shit

Dana

Europe will pull together

Jarron
we'll see

Dana
are you going to kill me?

Jarron
I am doing nothing
I might do something about the temperature, aren't
you cold?

Dana
this on my neck

Jarron
what about it?

Dana
what is it?

Jarron
it's nothing

Dana
why is it growing?

He shrugs.

Jarron
maybe you should go to a doctor

Dana
you put it there so that I would have to come back
to you
so I would come and find you

Jarron
here's the thing: I don't care

Dana
so you keep saying

Jarron
I care nothing about you
if I did before, it's gone now

Dana
so why are you here?

Jarron
I'm not.

Pause.

They look at each other.

He shrugs and looks at her again.

I'm not

He can't quite break away though. They stare at each other.

They are almost irresistibly drawn to each other.

Then the moment is broken.

Some music starts up in the background.

Jarron
what is that?

Dana
the next-door room

Jarron
can't you stop it?

Dana
probably not

Jarron
can't you ring down and get them to shut up?

Dana
what's wrong with it?

Jarron
it's music, it's fucking music

Dana
what is wrong with music?

Jarron
I don't like it, it plays with my head

Dana
you are by the telephone –

Jarron
alright

He picks up the telephone.

Dana comes and sits beside him, right at his back.

He arches his back to her touch.

Jarron
don't do that

Dana
it's in my head, I'm not doing anything

She twists and puts an arm around him.

He is drawn to her.

Jarron
I said stop

Dana
you stop

Jarron
you stop first

He can't stop himself.

He twists and grabs her.

It's unclear if he is holding her or hurting her.

They fight for a second.

They roll, they kiss.

For a second or two it's irresistible.

Then he breaks away.

> you can't have this
> you can't have this version of me
> this isn't how it is
> this isn't how I am
> you are fucking twisting with my head now

Dana
> turns out I am stronger than you.

Jarron
> sorry, not true

He slaps her.

She holds her face.

He slaps her again.

She slaps him.

He grabs her again.

She grabs him.

He looks at her.

He tries to look at her very soul.

He throws her down.

> I'm going
> you won't see me again

Dana
> so we can go back to normal, we can use our bank
> card?

Jarron

the banks have got nothing to do with me, I told you

Dana

bollocks

Jarron

goodbye, Dana

Dana

I don't think it's goodbye

Jarron

it will get pretty lonely, you know that.
pretty hard from here
you think you are cushioned, well, it is paper-thin.
Doesn't it feel draughty already?

Dana

someone will help us

Jarron

do you think?

Dana

as long as there are people there is some kind of
civilising influence

The demon laughs at that. Long and hard.

Dana

I'll keep looking for you

Jarron

you do that

Dana

this isn't over between you and me

He eats the chocolate.

don't eat the chocolate

He eats another bit.

we only have that for tomorrow

Jarron
you said bring it on

Dana
don't

He laughs again.

He eats more chocolate, and the bread.

Dana
don't touch the bread

Jarron
you'll have to tell her it was you.

Dana
leave her something.

He crams it into his mouth.

Jarron
why should I? I'm a god, I told you. I am the unclean.
The damned. I am the fucking nightmare.

Dana
where are you?
where will I find you?

He shrugs.

Jarron
I work for the UN

THIRTEEN

Dana is too hot in her bed.

The Librarian is giving her books. He is fanning himself.

Librarian

*How to Get to Sleep in a Room that is Now Too Hot.
How to Turn a Heating System Down in a Room
without Air Conditioning*. A classic actually. *How to
Get to Sleep Despite the Extreme Heat*. Very useful,
but the spine is a bit worn now. I could see if there is
another copy. Did you check to see if the windows
opened? Or perhaps this one. *How to Dream when
You Aren't Sure You Are Asleep*. *How to Stay Asleep
and Still Even if it Feels Like You Are in an Oven*, a
bit outdated but you could try it. *How to Ignore the
Sweat Running Down Your Face, Dry Eyes*. They're
really amazing these 'how to' books. They have got a
title for almost anything. *How to Lie Awake and Not
Breathe in the Air*

Dana

where's Jasmine?

Librarian

How to Wash in Hardly Any Water. Not particularly
recommended, but you never know

Dana

Jasmine?

Librarian

what to wear for a ten-mile trek. How to make a
water bottle from an old pair of socks, that doesn't
sound right –

Dana

where is Jasmine?

Librarian

how to find your sister
oh hang, wait a minute. There was one written just
like this
how to find your sister when she is in despair

Dana
why is she in despair?
OK so the food went but –
why is she in despair?

Librarian
it doesn't say.
it was just the title of a book. Do you want it or not?

Dana
I can't carry all these books.

Librarian
it's alright, that's why you have me. I carry them for
you.

Dana
why is Jasmine in despair?

Librarian
I don't have a title for that. Sorry.

FOURTEEN

Outside.

Jasmine is sitting on a bench.

Dana comes and sits beside her.

Dana
you could have left me a note
you could have left something to tell me where you
were going. I was worried. The room was so hot,
I woke up, no sign of you
went downstairs to see about the heat. No one at
reception.
went outside; nothing.
back to our room, worried now.
checked the toilet

Beat.

I know you are mad
you've a right to be but you didn't have to scare me
just shout, scream. I know that food was all we had,
and I know I have got at you for years for not being
able to control yourself –

Beat.

Dana
I don't know what came over me
I'm not sure I was actually awake
please don't be full of despair. We'll get some more
food
we'll find the embassy.

Jasmine
I'm not cross

Dana
you must be hungry, I mean I understand you have a
little person in there

Jasmine
I'm bleeding

Dana
what?

Jasmine
there's blood all over my pants

Dana
Jesus, when?

Jasmine
a few hours ago it started. The room got so airless,
I sat up in the bed
I felt something cool
I put my hand down

Dana
oh god

Jasmine
my blood was actually cooler than the room, I thought
what is this cool stuff on my thighs?

Dana
Jesus

Jasmine
so much of it
Dana, there was so much of it
then of course as more and more came it got hotter
only a tiny person, how could there be so much?

Dana
why are you sitting here, we need to get you help

Jasmine
I think it's gone

Dana
you don't know that

Jasmine
the amount of blood, I don't see –

Dana
stand up, you need some help

Jasmine
I don't know what to do, Dana, you'd think I would
know what to do

Dana
you haven't lost it yet
you just need some help that's all
you might just need a tablet

Jasmine
yes a tablet, maybe there's a tablet –

Dana

I'll get you a doctor

Jasmine

how will you get a doctor here?

Dana

there'll be a doctor

Jasmine

oh fucking hell –

Dana

you hang on, everything will be fine
we'll be telling that baby all about this one day I
promise.

Jasmine

it's starting to hurt

Dana

I need some help. Help. Let go of my hand, I'll go to
the hotel, they can ring a doctor. Stand up

Jasmine

I can't stand up

Dana

sit then, I won't be long –

FIFTEEN

Dana

No NO NO NO NO. Alright. Alright, you win.
Hands up. You are bigger than me. I got the message.
You win. I'll take your money, I'll do whatever. Don't
do this to Jasmine and her baby. This has nothing to
do with Jasmine.
oi, where are you? Come back.

I said I'll take your money.
it was just sex. Lust. Nothing happened.
the devil can't be tamed by love. You stay all powerful.
give me your fucking money.
where are you?
where are you?

A Woman is on the phone and talking to Dana.

Woman
I'm sorry I didn't catch that, what service do you
require?

Dana
ambulance.

Woman
it's a bad line, could you repeat?

Dana
ambulance. Ambulance, fucking ambulance

Woman
alright

Dana
how long before it gets here?

Woman
I need to do an assessment first

Dana
what sort of assessment? It's my sister, she's losing a
baby

Woman
is she breathing?

Dana
of course she is breathing, she is bleeding, that is the
thing

Woman
has she had a knock on the head?

Dana
no. Please just send the ambulance

Woman
chest pains?

Dana
she's losing a baby, didn't you hear me?

Woman
has she developed a headache or started slurring her words?

Dana
no, she is bleeding, she is bleeding a lot

The Librarian comes up to her with more tomes.

Librarian
How to Hold Your Sister's Hand when You Think She is Slipping Away.

Dana
I don't need a book, I just need an ambulance

Librarian
actually that is just a paper in a journal.

Woman
has she travelled overseas in the last three months?

Dana
no. No she hasn't.

Librarian
How to Count Someone's Heartbeat Even Though You Can Only Hear Your Own.

Woman
the ambulance is just being prepared

Dana

it doesn't need to be prepared, it just needs to get here

Librarian

are you still interested in these 'how to' books, sometimes I think they go too far.

Dana

give them to me

Woman

should be with you shortly

Dana

how shortly? How long will it take?

Librarian

How to Stay Calm in Moments of Duress. Rather straightforward to my mind, but nicely written

Dana

how to call the devil back, have you got that?

Woman

there's been an incident in the town centre, you're in a queue

Dana

what kind of queue?

Librarian

the e-books take a while, how are you spelling devil?

Dana

are you serious? Where is he? Get him back. I'll take his money

Librarian

How to Find an Ambulance in Hartenharten, no you have already done that

Woman

twenty minutes now

Dana

twenty minutes, there must be a way to call a devil

Librarian

you can't rush me

how to keep your cool when your sister is dying

Dana

she isn't dying

can you get it any quicker than twenty minutes?

Librarian

she doesn't get blood, she'll die

Dana

they'll give her blood then, won't they? Someone give
her some blood. Give me a book, how to make them
give someone blood when they need blood

Librarian

how to listen when people are talking nonsense

Dana

what sort of nonsense?

Woman

I am sorry I have to ask, do you have insurance?

Dana

insurance?

this is an emergency –

Librarian

how to keep your cool when life is stressful

Dana

– I don't need insurance

Woman

do you intend to pay for her treatment in cash?

Librarian

it's got a CD, this one with breathing exercises
meditation

Dana

Yes, we'll pay. I'll pay, whatever. I'll get you money.
I thought this was Europe

Woman

it is Europe but the hospital now only takes cash

Librarian

how to catch up with the times as they change

Dana

I don't have money on me. But I'll get it, I'll ring
someone.

Woman

do you still want the ambulance?

Dana

of course I want the ambulance. We have money in a
bank. We have money. Lots of money. Fucking hell,
demon, I'll take the money, please someone. Please
someone just help my sister. Please please please.
PLEASE.

SIXTEEN

Jasmine appears in a hospital gown.

Dana is waiting for her.

Jasmine starts to talk, serious and hard on herself.

Jasmine

I thought when it came to it, I would be good at it. I
thought I would find it all instinctive. I thought maybe
there would be this part of me that had been waiting
all these years, that would know exactly what to do.
But – hold on to it, that's the first thing isn't it? Rule
number one. You want to be a mother, hold on to it.
Seal it in, don't let it go all over the floor.

Dana

Jasmine –

Jasmine

that is kind of the first base, the easy slopes

Dana

listen to me

Jasmine

it's right that this happened.

Dana

no it isn't

Jasmine

I've got my head around it. I wasn't even sure that I
wanted it until today so it is fair enough.

Dana

come here –

Jasmine

I was stupid, see. If I had been one of the good
mothers, I would have told it I loved it. I would have
known it was precious. I would have put my knees
together, I would have taped myself up. Sat down
more. You should have made me do that. Why wasn't
I sitting? I could have stayed in bed. I shouldn't be here
with you, on this stupid trip, what was I thinking?
you have got to know how precious things are if you
want to hang on to them.

Dana

that isn't true

Jasmine

and if I was this stupid before, imagine how it could
have been after it was born? What if I still didn't
realise, and I then I forgot it and left it someplace?
Dana, what if I had gone on another jaunt with
you because I was dumb and left it someplace? And

then it got run over or stolen by wolves or kicked
about by ogres?
or what if I had picked it up wrong, because I still
didn't know, and I hurt its little neck? You know you
have to be careful of their little necks. What if I didn't
realise? What if I was listening to you going on and
not noticing what I was doing? What if the head fell
off? What if the neck snapped and the head fell off?
then I would have this headless baby, I would have this
horrible headless baby and what do you do with a
baby that doesn't have a head? I wouldn't have known
how to cuddle and comfort something like that. I
would get cross. I would shout at it because I was so
tired and it wouldn't feed. It would just bleed. Bleed
and bleed all over the floor. I would shake it. I would
hurt it, I would get very angry and shake it. Stop
bleeding I would say. Stop bleeding. You can't bleed
like this, you have to stop bleeding and live. You have
to live. You have to be my boy. You have to let me put
my arms around you and you have to grow up and ask
about the stars. You can't ask about the stars if you
are bleeding like this. You are just blood you aren't a
child. You put blood in a pot and make a pudding.
You mop it up with a sponge. You soak it up with
tissues and flush it down the loo. There is nothing to
you. You can't be my boy, my precious bundle of child,
you are just blood.
down the toilet you go. Blood.

Dana holds her.

Jasmine opens her mouth but can't make a sound.

SEVENTEEN

*Jasmine and Dana are by the roadside. They are in tatters
now.*

Dana is trying to hitch a lift.

The Librarian is with them but sitting a little way back.

Dana
I think it will get easier now.

Librarian
really?

Dana
yes
we have hit rock bottom.
let's face it, it can't be much worse than this.
we lost everything.
every single thing we had, we lost. Didn't we?
we even lost the suitcase that held everything we had.
whatever happens now, it can't be as bad.

Librarian
it's Monday

Dana
I know that

Librarian
I'm just saying that it is technically, it is Monday
lunchtime and you are nowhere near Alexandria

Beat.

Dana
maybe I can speak to them on the phone. You can
rearrange these things. When we tell them what has
happened to us on our journey they will understand.

Librarian
of course they will.

Beat.

you sold your phone to pay for Jasmine's treatment

Dana
I know I sold my phone
do you have to tell me everything that I already know?

Librarian
so how are you going to call?

Dana
I'll work it out

Librarian
there aren't many phone boxes that are working

Dana
I said I'll work it out

Librarian
and anyway you need a coin

Dana
thank you so much

Librarian
do you want a book to help you?

Dana
no thanks

Librarian
sure?

Dana
absolutely
no fucking books

Librarian
you have to go through lots of countries to get to
Alexandria, so anyway even if you do manage to make
a call –

Dana
we can go through lots of countries

Librarian

the borders are shut. Istanbul has shut its borders one
way, Alexandria the other
all of Europe is trying to get out

Dana

they'll let us through

Librarian

you think
why you?

Dana

I have a presentation to give. When I explain they will
let us through

Librarian

it's quite different over there. Better
of course everyone wants to get through

Dana

well that means when we get there, things will be
easier
when we get there

Librarian

when you call them maybe you should ask them for
some kind of identification. Something that says they
invited you
I'm just thinking ahead

Dana

OK I'll ask them

Beat.

do you think there are going to be any cars coming by
this way? when did you last see a car?

Librarian

why do you want a car, you won't get a lift.

Dana
is there anything constructive you could say?

Librarian
Jasmine is anaemic.
she needs some iron.

Dana
I know that.

Beat.

Librarian
I'm just saying if you don't get her some help soon,
parts of her will start to fail –

Dana
could you look it up on a database, when did the last
car drive past on this particular piece of road?

Librarian
here?

Dana
yes

Librarian
alright

Dana
I saw people begging.
I saw a pile of people –

Librarian
I didn't see that

Dana
well, you were looking the wrong way
haven't you got a book about it?

Librarian
extreme poverty, yes. I believe I have

Dana
the sort where you have to sell your children?

Librarian
yes, there are various titles in that series

Dana
what are they called?

Librarian
there are lots of them, volumes and volumes
new ones coming out all the time. Do you want a new
release?

Dana
back there. There was a tiny little toddler they put out
to do the begging for them.

Librarian
that's probably a story told in an appendix somewhere

Dana
they didn't even do the begging themselves.

Librarian
common these days

Dana
I went up to the toddler and asked him where his
parents were, but they weren't there. They just left him
on the road

Librarian
maybe they had other things to do

Dana
what other things?
he was their toddler
what other things are there?

Librarian
I don't know.

I'm sure I have got a book about other things that
people might be doing

Dana
how could they have left him there. Right by the
roadside?

Librarian
don't ask me

Dana
that doesn't happen
no one does that.

Librarian
look around you.
do you recognise a single thing any more?

Dana looks around.

Dana
maybe it wasn't their toddler

Librarian
maybe.

Beat.

Dana
is there a guidebook to this place?

Librarian
there is a guidebook to every place.

Dana
what is it called here then?

Librarian
I don't think it has a name.

Dana
it's hell then
it might have been Europe yesterday.

I asked the man in the shop if he would give me some water. I asked the woman by the tap. I just want some water

Librarian
technically the water situation is complicated, and a bit political

Dana
it's really fucking screwed, isn't it?
there was nothing in the shop because everyone had gone crazy and grabbed it for themselves. The police aren't being paid any more so they don't care. They are doing most of the grabbing. You ask someone to help you they will just knife you.

Beat.

people did use to care, didn't they? We didn't just imagine it.

Librarian
they did use to, yes

Beat.

to cut a long story short. There's no petrol in the pumps, of course there are no cars. I don't have a book but a very nicely written article about it. With photos. There is hardly any petrol in most of the old eurozone countries so people have started to use a bicycle.
the bicycle has made a resurgence
those that have one

Dana
where the fuck will I get a bicycle from?

Librarian
I am not saying you should get a bicycle, I am just saying people are resilient. They use what they have

Dana
this is resilience?

Beat.

what am I going to do with her?

Librarian
I can't carry her. I've got all the books
can she walk?

Dana
I don't know.

She sits down next to Jasmine.

were you asleep?

Jasmine
maybe a little

Dana
we need to try to get to the border. Then we can still
get to the presentation.
If I can do the presentation I can get the job. I can get
the job, I can get us out of this.

Jasmine
will they have a place where I can rest?

Dana
yes, I think that is exactly what they'll have

Jasmine
after the presentation?

Dana
exactly.

Jasmine
we don't have any money
don't you need money to get to the border?

Dana
I don't think so

Librarian
technically, you do

Dana
please shut up.

Jasmine
you do need money, Dana

Dana
alright, but don't worry about it, I'll get us some money. I'll get a short-term loan if necessary, we can pay it back when I get the job.

Jasmine
you can't get a loan

Dana
I'll get a loan
can you stand up?

Jasmine
when we see the doctor we could ask him to check the baby as well. Could we?

Dana
the baby?

Librarian
you didn't tell her?

Dana
I did tell her

Jasmine
do you think there are still doctors?

Dana
you lost the baby, love

Jasmine
no

Dana
Jasmine honey, you lost the baby.

Beat.

Jasmine
don't be silly, that's just a joke

Dana
no

Jasmine
no?

Dana
sorry.

Jasmine
oh yes. I lost the baby. I keep forgetting.
silly of me to forget something like that. Just when it
comes, when we have it in our arms?
we won't put it out to beg for us, would we?

Dana
but we won't

Jasmine
no, we won't

Beat.

Dana
I mean we wouldn't even if we could

Jasmine
what?

Dana
we haven't got the baby any more. The baby was just
blood

Jasmine
are you sure?

Dana
I'm sure

Jasmine
you always say the meanest things. I don't know whether to believe you. Why won't we have it in our arms?

Dana
Jasmine sweetheart –

Jasmine
I know I know it's gone.
you said it's gone. I just have to keep remembering.
why can't I keep remembering?

Dana
please stay strong

Jasmine
I am strong

Dana
I have to get you to the border

Librarian
you need money to get to the border

Dana
will you stop saying that –
I know we haven't got money but we'll get some

Jasmine
I don't even want to go to the border. I'm happy here, in the dust
can't I just lie down here and forget about it all.

Dana
I don't think you should do that.

Beat.

Sit up. Sit up, Jaz
you remember how you always looked after me, and
you always had this strength whatever happened, you
could be steady, and stable and –

Jasmine
let me lie down –

Dana (*to the Librarian*)
can you look after her?
while I go and get some money

Librarian
yes

Dana
just make sure no one hurts her

Librarian
you said you wouldn't

Dana
I know what I said

Librarian
he will have won

Dana
he has won. He has reduced us to nothing. He won.
look at us, he fucking won.
will you look after her or not?

Librarian
you'll need some books

Dana
I don't need books

Librarian
I think you should have them, there are things that are
going to help you in these books

Dana
like what?

Librarian
taking your clothes off in front of a stranger

Dana
I've done that before

Librarian
The Economics of Selling Oneself

Dana
hardly

Librarian
How to Look Like You Are Enjoying Something while Your Skin Is Repelled

Dana
OK I'll take that.

Librarian
How to Stop Gagging with Someone's Putrid Penis in Your Mouth
I think you should take this one too.
How to Make Sure You Don't Get Strangled. How to Not Get a Disease that Will Kill You. How to Stay Alive during Prostitution.

She takes the books.

one final one, *How to Forget the Whole Thing Once It Is Over*

Dana
I won't forget the whole thing

Librarian
there are some really good books on self-meditation. Self-hypnosis. Letting everything go.

Dana
    look after my beautiful sister Jasmine. Would you
    please do that?

EIGHTEEN

*Dana lifts her clothes up, rips at them to make herself
look more alluring.*

*A man comes along. He throws a blanket and a horrible
old pillow on the floor.*

Dana tries to pin him down on price before they start.

Dana
    my price is 45 euros.

Punter
    you have to be kidding

Dana
    45 euros and I'll give you a good time

Punter
    have you done this before?

Dana
    yes

Punter
    only a line like that, people don't use it.

Dana
    do you want to do this or not?

Punter
    of course, but a 'good time', don't say that. And 45
    euros, sorry to say, 45 euros and you get someone a bit
    more –

Dana
what?

Punter
well-kept, don't want to be rude but
someone whose hair doesn't look like it is already
falling out.

Dana
25 then

Punter
15

Dana
that's too little, you don't know what I am giving you

Punter
I am pretty sure I do
I am pretty sure I know exactly.

Dana
I have a sister who isn't well, I have to get her out of
here

Punter
we all have to get out of here.
you think everyone isn't desperate to get out of this
place?
15 or nothing

Dana
17

Punter
sorry not interested

Dana
alright. 15

He laughs.

Punter
how about 10?

Dana
you just said 15

Punter
I like this, aren't you enjoying this bit?

Dana
devil, is this you?

Punter
what?

Dana
if this is a game –

Punter
I thought we were talking about a price

Dana
we are. Ten.

Punter
let's see what you've got then.

Dana starts to take off her clothes. She is embarrassed.

Dana
will you take off your clothes too?

Punter
eventually.

Dana
only I feel a bit –

Punter
you really aren't used to this, are you?

Beat.

Dana takes her shirt off.

Underneath the birthmark is all over her.

Punter
  what's wrong with you?

Dana
  nothing

Punter
  that mark all over you, what is it?

Dana
  it's just a birthmark
  I was born with it.

Punter
  never seen a birthmark like that before.

He comes towards her.

  does it hurt?

Dana
  no

Punter
  it's like a tattoo
  I like it.

Dana
  do you?

Punter
  what do you do?

Dana
  what do you want?

Punter
  I want everything. All ways.
  don't worry, when you see what I've got, you'll have
  a smile on your face

She kisses him.

  more

She starts to caress him through his clothes.

more

She unzips his trousers.

more

She takes his cock into her mouth.

He grabs her hair and pulls her back.

He pulls up her skirt, violent suddenly, and enters her.

The sex is brutal, almost rape.

It hurts her.

It hurts her more and more with every thrust.

Dana tries to stand up, she talks to the Interviewers.

Dana
for my presentation I wanted to speak about the
customer experience. How the customer experience
can affect the moment of money transfer. If the
customer has been satisfied, then the handing over of
money can prove more

She finds it difficult to continue.

it can prove more . . .

She is sore, she has been brutally treated.

if the encounter has been seen to be a good one then
the customer –

She looks about her.

why won't you talk to me any more?
where are you? Devil, I know you are still there

The lights from the interview come on.

Dana
is that you?

Interviewer 1
Ms Edwards?

Dana
oh

Interviewer 2
can you hear us?

Dana
yes

Interviewer 1
we were expecting you last Monday.

Dana
I'm sorry about that

Interviewer 3
is that all you have to say?

Dana
I got held up

Interviewer 2
if we are to hold this research grant for you –

Dana
I'll be there

Interviewer 3
when, Ms Edwards?

Dana
as soon as I can.
can you help me get to the border?

Interviewer 2
we leave travel arrangements up to the individuals. We
understand that this is a difficult time for those coming
from the European Union, but –

Dana
they have more or less closed the border into Turkey,
and if we go by boat –

Interviewer 3
we are sure you will find a way

Dana
there is no way.
all the borders are shut

Interviewer 1
we'll leave it open for a week.

Dana
could you give me a piece of paper saying that you
have invited me?

Interviewer 1
we aren't really sure

Interviewer 3
the administrative burden

Dana
if you could give me a piece of paper saying that I have
a position to go to

Interviewer 2
but you don't have a position. That is just the matter
that we are discussing.

Interviewer 3
you might have a position

Dana
there are thousands of people ahead of me
even if they reopen the borders

Interviewer 3
are you saying you want to cancel, Ms Edwards?

Beat.

Interviewer 1
there are plenty of others we could fill this post with.

Dana
no

Interviewer 2
you'll be here?

Dana
I'll be there

Interviewer 1
we'll see you soon then.

The voices seem to go. Dana is left alone in the space.

Dana
devil?

She stands in the bright light.

I can tell you are there.
you are everywhere now. I can feel you. Hear you.
you are in every face. Every carcass that was a person.
You are in the looters and the loan sharks. The
racketeers and the lost.
you might as well reveal yourself.
have your victory.
enjoy the last laugh

Beat.

you have had it all. What more is there?

Dana is still having sex with the Punter.

He comes to a noisy climax.

Thank god it is over.

The man zips his trousers back up.

He gets some money out of his wallet, that he carefully puts on the ground next to her.

Punter
thank you. That was nice.

Then he goes.

Dana is left alone.

Dana
oh god.

She is bruised and broken.

She just about manages to sit up.

She cries out once or twice. He really hurt her.

She gathers up the money.

A woman comes along. She is wearing tattered clothes that perhaps once looked smart.

Marta
hello?

Dana
hello.

Marta
you look hurt, are you OK?

Dana
not really

There is a second woman behind her. She is also covered in dirt.

Clara
what's up with her?

Marta
I'm not sure

Dana
  I'll be alright

Marta
  you look bruised

Clara
  only this is kind of where we are

Dana
  what?

Clara
  this whole park

Marta
  give her a minute

Clara
  why?

Marta
  she's hurt

Clara
  we're all hurt
  aren't you hurt? Fuck, who isn't hurt?

Dana
  I'm sorry I didn't realise

Marta
  it isn't marked out

Dana
  I thought it was just a park

Clara
  far as those trees, back to the path. Ours. Past the
  swings down to the road

Dana
  OK

Clara
if you want the bit behind the car park you have to
fight one of the girls over there for it, good luck to you

Dana
I don't want to fight.

Marta
they used to be primary school teachers but you
wouldn't know it now

Dana
I'm going

Clara
how much did you make out of interest?

Marta
let her go

Clara
I'm just asking

Dana
not much really

Dana picks up her bits and pieces and starts to move

Clara
go on let us look
we know how it works, we can help you
see if you could get more next time

Dana
there won't be a next time

Clara
let me see

Dana isn't sure whether to trust them.

Marta
we know what this is like
we're the same as you

She shows them, her hand still shaking.

Marta
   not bad
   horrible isn't it?

Clara
   it doesn't matter how it is –

Marta
   don't be brutal

Clara
   she has to understand, we've got nothing else, only this
   place and ourselves

Dana
   what?

Marta
   she used to be a lawyer

Clara
   it's about fairness

Dana
   I told you, I didn't know this place was yours

Clara
   thing is, you can't not know things any more. You
   can't stumble.

Dana
   I'm going

Marta
   if we had any choice

Clara
   it's a jungle now, the girls over there, the ones that way

Dana
   my sister has just lost a baby, and she needs to be
   treated

Clara

she needs, you need. Who is talking about need
anyway? It's a useless term. Everyone needs
I've got a mother who's dying, she's got three daughters

Marta

hand it over, make it easy

Dana

I know you

Marta

don't be stupid

Dana

you used to be on the telly –
you used to read the news

Marta

hey – there's no problem here

Dana

what happened to you?

Clara takes the money. She passes it to Marta.

Clara

you want to save your sister? Grow some teeth

Dana

what did say?

Dana finds the strength of a warrior.

She rushes at Clara, savage for a second.

Clara

oi

Clara is savage back.

give that here –

Dana

it's mine

Marta is savage too.

Dana
fuck you, I earned it

Marta
does it matter?

Dana attacks them. She gets the money back.

They turn on her.

They are more brutal and there are two of them.

Marta speaks aloud as she thumps her.

Marta
this is not personal. We told you. We need it, that's all.

Dana loses and is kicked repeatedly.

The women take her money.

They kick her again, just to make sure.

Dana is left beaten up like a piece of meat.

Clara
it's OK, she's got a fanny hasn't she? She can use it
again

NINETEEN

The boat.

*Jasmine and Dana are on a boat. With them on the boat
are hundreds of other people. They are jammed in like
sardines.*

Jasmine
do you think we should ring our local politician?

Dana
what?

Jasmine
well, someone must still be trying to make things a bit
better

Dana
I don't think the politicians are still working

Jasmine
of course they are
they always say on the telly you can ring them
only there are so many people we have to ring them
before everyone else does, everybody is grabbing, you
get there first

Dana
where?

Jasmine
to the telephone.
ooh god

Dana
it's alright, just a wave

Jasmine
the politicians will be getting aid from other countries,
we can tell them how to spend it, they will thank us
probably

Dana
what aid?

Jasmine
from all those countries that we used to give aid to.
African countries

Dana
we gave a bit to
we didn't give very much

Jasmine
it's their turn to help us now, they can't just watch
was that another wave?

Dana
yes I think so

Jasmine
do I even like boats?

Dana
try to like them

Jasmine
there should be a roof. Tell the politician that when
you get to the phone. A boat with this number of
people –
they said they would only take eighty, this must be
over three hundred

Dana
they do this run every night, it'll be fine

Jasmine
oh god

Dana
another wave, a bit of swell

Jasmine
they should sail in the day, if you could see the waves
coming you could get ready for them

Dana
I think it has to be at night
so no one sees

Jasmine
did we have to pay for this?

Dana
don't worry about the money

Jasmine
I do worry about the money.

Beat.

it's an outrage, this should be a free service. People like
us need to be saved. And crammed in like this. Treated
like sardines.
it hasn't even got seats for us all
we would need a seat for the baby if we still had it.
Tell the politician that, there aren't even baby seats.
Don't worry, I am remembering that we lost the baby,
but even still –

Dana
I guess it is what makes it worth their while. They are
taking a risk after all

Jasmine
we are taking a risk
this boat should have been rebuilt years ago
maybe we should try and get near an edge, then if
anything happens we can try and grab one of the life
rings.

Dana
we can't move
I don't think we should try and move now

Jasmine
did you say if I liked boats?

Dana
I said you loved them

Jasmine
I feel quite sick

Dana
you'll be fine
hang on to my hand.

Jasmine hangs on to Dana's hand.

Jasmine
if the baby was here we would have to hang on to it

very tight. make sure it didn't go near the edge. This
would be a terrible journey with a baby

Dana
you remember that we lost the baby?

Jasmine
of course I do.
I was just telling the baby we lost it. It's a naughty
baby, keeps forgetting.
there is nothing wrong with me

Dana
I know

Jasmine
will they be glad to see us when we get to Alexandria?

Dana
maybe

Jasmine
I hope so. All this way.
I want a clean bed with clean sheets

Dana
granted

Jasmine
a house with a back yard, maybe a swing

Dana
OK

Jasmine
fresh water out of a tap, bread
just like at home
shoes that don't make my feet bleed

Dana
once I get the job, it will all be sorted

Jasmine
we won't ever be going back home, will we?

Dana
I don't think there is anything left for us there.

Beat.

Jasmine
I don't like the idea of not existing.
of being a person but not a person. Like the baby

Dana
the baby –

Jasmine
is dead I know, whereas we –
we'll just be illegal. I understand.

Dana
when we get there, it will get better.
it will all feel better

There is a sudden jolt.

Jasmine
what was that?

Dana
what?

Jasmine
that bump

Dana
we're out on the open sea, there are bound to be some bumps

Jasmine
I wish I could swim

Dana
if anything goes wrong, you grab a life ring

Jasmine
 what about the baby?

Dana
 we don't have the baby remember

Jasmine
 oh yes, I forgot again. Silly baby made me forget.
 they're greedy the people who run this ship. There's no
 cover, not enough life-jackets, nowhere to sit

Dana
 it doesn't matter how we get there, we just get there
 OK?

Jasmine
 OK.

The Librarian comes and taps Dana on the shoulder.

Dana
 not now

Librarian
 you'll need a book

Dana
 I don't want a book
 I am getting out of this. When we are there

Librarian
 Rough Crossings for the Weak in Spirit

Dana
 we aren't weak in spirit
 I need to hold my sister's hand

Librarian
 OK, *How to Spot Danger and Do Something about It*

Dana
 we aren't in danger
 the sea is alright, it's a short crossing, we go via Crete

Librarian

How to Spot Rocks in the Dark

Dana

there aren't any rocks

Librarian

How to Spot Rocks You Can't See, though technically this is a guide to navigational techniques and this boat doesn't have any, so –

Dana

this boat doesn't have any?

Librarian

they have a compass and some other stuff
I might have a book on that.
oh, people are puking, do you want something on how to stop getting covered in vomit in an open-aired vessel?

Dana

not really.

Librarian

OK.
How to Hold Your Breath for a Very Long Time

Dana

I don't need to hold my breath, why would I need to hold my breath?

Librarian

you need to hold your breath for a very long time, Dana

Dana

I am out in the air, I don't need to hold my breath
see, I am breathing

Librarian

hold your breath now, Dana
hold your breath for a very long time

The interview lights come back on.

Dana is drenched, and standing there sopping wet.

Interviewer 1
Ms Edwards

Dana
yes

Interviewer 1
you seem not to be breathing.

Dana
I am breathing.
I'm holding my breath

Interviewer 1
you seem to be going under

Dana
I'm not going under

Interviewer 2
if this means you can't give your presentation, this will
cause us no end of headache

Dana
I'll give my presentation

Interviewer 2
you seem to be still, Ms Edwards

Dana
I'm not still

Interviewer 1
you seem to be being pulled under, there are others
screaming but you don't seem to be one of them

Dana
I'm screaming but it's hard when you are holding your
breath

Interviewer 1
no words are coming.

Interviewer 3
Ms Edwards

Dana
I'm holding my breath, how can words be coming out
of my mouth

Interviewer 2
you needed to hold your breath earlier

Dana
I'm holding it now

Interviewer 1
the water as you hit it caused you shock

Interviewer 3
you got swept away, you hit your head

Dana
no that is not right
I'm holding my breath
I'm holding my breath
I'm holding my breath.

.

TWENTY

The demon is behind Dana.

He picks her up and carries her like a small child.

She is inert.

And soaking wet. Hair bedraggled.

He is dressed in uniform. He works for the UN.

*As he carries her forward a trolley is brought. A rough-
and-ready hospital is created.*

The demon puts Dana on the hospital trolley.

A woman Doctor comes and checks her over.

Jarron
she was a migrant

Doctor
we don't have her name?

Jarron
I don't think so, no

Doctor
well I doubt anyone will bother with dental records.
We'll just put 'unknown woman' on the death
certificate. Cause of death?

Jarron
drowning and hypothermic shock
the electrolytes in her blood

Doctor
she held her breath for too long.

Jarron
basically
the trauma to the head might have killed her first
if she was lucky

The Doctor looks her over.

Doctor
well, if you will be stupid enough to cross on a boat
like that
they bring it on themselves
what is this mark on her?

Jarron
I think it was the lack of oxygen as she went down

Doctor
strange, I haven't seen one like that before. How many
have we got?

Jarron

this is the ninety-third, but they are still pulling them out of the water

Doctor

why do they do it?
why do they take the risk?

Beat.

Jarron

what should we do with the body?

Doctor

we'll organise some kind of burial. See, that is our problem too. We either bury them here or pay to have them shipped back to where they came from. Either way it comes to us to fork out. The economics of the European collapse will go on and on.

The Doctor starts to go off.

get her processed and get on to the other ones. Don't spend too long

The devil sits beside Dana.

He puts his hand on her cheek.

He touches her gently across her body.

He lifts her up and sits behind her.

He cradles her.

The Librarian comes in.

Jarron

what are you doing?

Librarian

what are you doing?

The devil doesn't have an answer to that.

Librarian
I was just delivering some books

Jarron
I don't think she needs books now

Librarian
on the contrary, she needs lots of books.
where she is going, it gets even more complicated.

Jarron
you weren't a good guide
look what happened to her

Librarian
you did this, not me

Jarron
I didn't do a single thing

Librarian
alright, but you watched. You didn't stop it.

Jarron
she was naive. She had to see a thing or two

Beat.

shall I wake her?

Beat.

do you want me to wake her?

Librarian
you can't wake her
technically she is dead

Jarron
technically, her heart is still beating. Faintly but it's
present. She could go either way in truth.
on the one hand, a shot of adrenaline and eyes open.
Some oxygen perhaps if she needs it. On the other,

just leave her on a trolley and it will be over in an
hour or so.

The demon takes a small syringe out of his pocket.

I have it right here
the two gates

Librarian
don't wake her

Jarron
why not?

Librarian
her sister also died.
I just think one without the other
she has been through enough, this little body

Jarron
she deserved it. She thought she could make me love
her, how wrong she was.

He lifts the ampule of adrenaline.

The Librarian stops him.

Jarron
you are only supposed to advise, you aren't supposed
to do anything. You are the librarian, you stay in your
corner

Librarian
even the corner man can stand up

Jarron
oh can he?

Librarian
she has been through enough, I said let it stop

The demon deliberates.

Jarron
and let her go?

Librarian
she's got nothing left, after all, has she? You proved
your point

Jarron
she has got everything. What do you mean, nothing?
she made it over the crossing. She made it to this side.
We could wake her up. Give her some clothes. She
could do her presentation, get the job, decent salary,
buy a flat
she is one of the lucky ones
she could have everything
how can you say she has got nothing?

Librarian
but her eyes are open now, as you said, she can't shut
them again. Even you can't shut them. What she has
seen – she thought that men and women were basically
good, human nature in essence benign. Then she saw it
wash all away, one crisis and the jungle came at her,
she heard the hyenas howling, saw hell etched on
other people's faces. Let's face it, she saw the dark
swamp at the bottom of the human soul and once you
have seen that –

Jarron
we make her forget then.
easy
we make her forget.
we put her in a trance, we wash it off. She is as good
as dead, we wash her in the river between the two
worlds if we have to.

The devil starts to take off Dana's soaked clothes.

Librarian
how can you forget all that?

157

Jarron
　you can forget anything
　stop making so much of it, so people get a bit nasty,
　people like Dana they live in a hazy afternoon.
　Pleasant but fragile, one slip through a crack –
　if you dance on the cracks, after all, one day you'll fall
　through, that has to be a saying. Has someone
　important said that?
　pass me those shoes, those shoes will suit her

The Librarian passes the shoes.

　and a jacket I have laid over that chair

The Librarian passes the jacket.

He starts to put new clothes on her.

Modern clothes, clothes that she will look good in.

　I'm going to wake her
　you haven't been a good guide.
　I am going to wake her.
　find her a book

Librarian
　like what?

Jarron
　a book on modern living. A book that might have
　'modern living' in the title. I don't know. *How to
　Furnish a Flat in a Weekend? What to Wear when You
　Want to Look Good. The Cinema Guide.* A cookery
　book. A manual on which over-expensive car to buy.
　*How to Get a Good Seat at the Theatre. Which
　Charity You Should Give to to Make you Feel Better.
　What to Say on a First Date. Topiary for Beginners,
　The Low-Carb Diet, How to Write a Novel, To Floss
　or Not to Floss.*
　do you want me to go on?

He pulls Dana's hair back.

What Not to Wear, Social Media, Twitter, Pastry-
Making for Chefs, Meditation for People who Do Too
Much, The Work–Life Balance and How to Survive It

He washes her face.

To Smack or Not to Smack, History for Idiots, A
Guide to Alsace Wine, Beating Anxiety, Overcoming
Insomnia, Sinusitis, The Prostate Conundrum, How to
Chose a Wig, A Thousand Things to See before You
Die

*He gets her to stand up. Her eyes are still shut. But she
stands by herself.*

Jarron
Dana
Dana

The lights come on.

*The voices of the interview panel join in with the calling
of her name.*

Dana.
Dana.
Dana.

The interview lights come on.

*Dana is standing there, now fully restored in smart
clothes suitable for an interview.*

Dana wakes with a sharp intake of breath.

Interviewer 1
if you would like to start your presentation now.